PIERRE DELION ON PSYCHOPOLITICS

PIERRE DELION ON PSYCHOPOLITICS

"What Is Institutional Psychotherapy?"

&

"The Republic of False Selves"

Pierre Delion

Translated by Matthew H. Bowker

First published in 2023 by
Phoenix Publishing House Ltd
62 Bucknell Road
Bicester
Oxfordshire OX26 2DS

Copyright © 2023 to Matthew H. Bowker for the translation, translator notes, and arrangement of material.

Copyright © 2018 to Éditions d'une, Paris, for the original essays by Pierre Delion.

The right of Pierre Delion to be identified as the author of this work has been asserted in accordance with §§ 77 and 78 of the Copyright Design and Patents Act 1988.

All rights reserved. No part of this publication may be reproduced, stored in a retrieval system, or transmitted, in any form or by any means, electronic, mechanical, photocopying, recording, or otherwise, without the prior written permission of the publisher.

British Library Cataloguing in Publication Data

A C.I.P. for this book is available from the British Library

ISBN-13: 978-1-800131-46-0

Typeset by Medlar Publishing Solutions Pvt Ltd, India

www.firingthemind.com

Contents

About the author   vii
About the translator   ix
Translator's introduction   xi

What Is Institutional Psychotherapy?   1

The Republic of False Selves   49

Index   113

About the author

Pierre Delion is professor emeritus of child psychiatry at the University of Lille, former chief of the Lille University Hospital Center Child Psychiatry Department, and a psychoanalyst. He has worked extensively with autism, psychosis, and all archaic pathologies, and with babies. He has led several teams of "sectoral psychiatry," including one in a university hospital, and has focused on combining sectoral psychiatry with institutional psychotherapy in an attempt to encourage humane psychiatric practices. He has written numerous psychiatric works about babies, autism, psychosis, and institutional psychotherapy, and has created an institute of psychoanalytic psychotherapy for children and adolescents in Lille. He continues to promote humane psychiatry by participating in experience exchange meetings with numerous teams in the health and medico-social sectors, and by giving lectures on psychiatry.

He insists on the need not to oppose the neurosciences to transferential psychopathology, but, on the contrary, to use these contributions so as to take into account all the anthropological factors involved in psychic suffering.

About the translator

Matthew H. Bowker, Ph.D., was educated at Columbia University, Institut d'études politiques de Paris, and the University of Maryland, College Park. He is the author of over fifteen books and several dozen journal articles and chapters on psychopolitical theory. He is currently Clinical Assistant Professor in the Social Sciences Interdisciplinary Program at The State University of New York (SUNY).

Translator's introduction

Matthew H. Bowker

Pierre Delion is professor emeritus in child psychiatry in the faculty of medicine at Lille, a child psychiatrist, and a psychoanalyst. His work is as straightforward as it is affecting. Sadly, he is not read enough in the English-speaking world, not because his teaching, writings, and political activities are altogether unknown to us, but rather because his works have not yet been translated into English. The present book attempts to address this unfortunate deficit in our knowledge.

Delion's words have been easy to translate into English with only the rarest exceptions, to be discussed below. Apart from the translation of his books' terminology, it has been important to me as a translator to remain as faithful as possible to the original meaning of Delion's words while, at the same time, attempting to convey something of his style, which combines a careful thoughtfulness with the power and urgency that can only come from a scholar-practitioner with vast experience and understanding. Of course, as any humble translator will tell you, if one wants the unadulterated Pierre Delion, one must read him in the original French.

A term used in *The Republic of False Selves* may cause readers some confusion. That term is "*socius*," which, in the Latin, refers to a singular associate or confidant, as in: "Mr. Jones was a long-time assistant and *socius* of the President." Those familiar with the work of Gilles Deleuze may recognize the term *socius* in his specific usage, referring to that to which production is attributed, for example, the body of the despot in empire; capital under capitalism. For Delion, however, the term takes on broader meaning to include the entire social, cultural, organizational, and familial environment of an individual or group of individuals, such that it comes to refer to the environmental context of a patient as well as what we might think of as the collective social psyche of a population.

At the same time, while American scholars, in particular, have been a bit obsessed by Hannah Arendt's famous distinction between *social* and *political* realms of action, Delion finds no such clear division. In fact, his work challenges this construction at its root, arguing that it is precisely the *liens sociétaux* (which I have translated as "*social bonds*") through which we attend to each other as subjects that make true democracy possible. Here, of course, we are talking not about democracy as the simple act of voting (although Delion's wise discussion of media-effects on voting should not be discounted here) but of a broader conception of democracy as a state of politics in which each individual may come to realize maturity in a society that respects, rather than alienates, his humanity.

In Delion's own words, democracy refers to a "society based on freedom and equality ... or more generally still, to a set of values: political, social, or cultural ideals and principles."

These democratic values and principles are the same as those needed in social organizations and institutions of care for the mentally ill. Indeed, he notes in *The Republic of False Selves*: "What holds for person-to-person psychiatry also holds true for democracy." This book, in particular, moves quickly and is quite rich, as it begins with politics, turns deftly to media criticism, examines deleterious social and political developments on the field of psychiatry, and finally returns to a discussion of politics.

Readers should note well that the two texts presented here were not originally intended to be paired together, so the reader may find that he or she must do a bit of work in moving from one to the other. In my view, the works operate quite well as a duo, connecting the micro- to the macro- of psychopolitics, from the individual symptom to the world's democratic movements. In deciding which text to present first, the author and I have opted to begin with *What Is Institutional Psychotherapy?* "Institutional psychotherapy" is referred to at times within the text as "I.P." This term (and this abbreviation) may well be unfamiliar to American or UK readers, just as its concomitant, "sector psychiatry," refers to a manner, operant since the 1960s in France, of organizing mental health care around specific geographic areas with the goal of providing care to patients within their immediate *socius* and by professionals familiar with and even operating in the same *socius*. Delion's argument in *What Is Institutional Psychotherapy?* is (at the very least) twofold:

(1) The "institution" must be regarded as the entirety of human, psychic, and social work that informs the care of the patient and therefore contributes to his or her "transferential constellation," and
(2) The institution and all of its constituents (i.e., persons and professionals performing any function) must be held, cared for, and listened to as much as the administrators of the institution, if it is to be maximally humane and effective.

We believe this book affords the reader an introduction to Delion's thought within the field of psychotherapy before asking readers to explore the broader political connections between the clinical institution and the society as a whole in *The Republic of False Selves*.

WHAT IS INSTITUTIONAL PSYCHOTHERAPY?
A Conversation with Yasuo Miwaki

Pierre Delion

Original publication details

Qu'est-ce que la psychothérapie institutionnelle? Conversation avec Yasuo Miwaki by Pierre Delion

Printed in France, at the ISIPRINT printing house (Saint-Denis) in May 2018.

Legal deposit: May 2018

© Éditions d'une, Paris, 2018

All reproduction, translation and adaptation rights reserved for all countries.

This edition translated and reproduced with the kind permission of the publisher.

"The least we can do is to hope that something can serve as a support to the subject, confirming the phoric function for which any institution worthy of the name is responsible."

"And in such perspective, this something may become 'animated' and may support an animist vision of the world: even if Westerners deny themselves to be animists, their vision of the world is permanently caught up in the transferential movement with the things of the surrounding world."

Contents

Note on the present work   7

1. Establishments and institutions   9

2. Active therapy   13
   2.1. Insanity and social alienation   14
   2.2. Multireferential transference and dissociated transference   15
   2.3. What is a transferential constellation?   17
   2.4. Transferential constellations and organizational difficulties   17
   2.5. Projective identification and adhesive identification   18

3. Institutional psychotherapy and antipsychiatry   23

4. Transversality and institutional analysis   27

5. The welcoming function   31

6. Continuity of care   35

7. The flesh, the thing   39

8. Deinstitutionalize?   41

9. Sector psychiatry   43

10. Work and adaptation   45

Note on the present work

Dr. Yasuo Miwaki recently asked me to come to Japan to hold a conference on *Institutional Psychotherapy*, which he had discovered during an internship at the clinic in La Borde in 1998. Since then, he remained in contact with Jean Oury, and was deeply affected by the latter's death in May 2014.

On the occasion of the publication of *Mon combat pour une psychiatrie humaine*,[1] he hoped that I could answer a few questions that arose while reading this book. These questions formed the backbone of the conference that was delivered in Tokyo on November 11, 2017, and which he translated into Japanese.

---

[1] P. Delion (with P. Coupechoux), *Mon combat pour une psychiatrie humaine*. Paris: Albin Michel, 2016.

I cannot thank him enough for his role in disseminating the concepts of institutional psychotherapy in his country, as well as in the Scientific Society of Transcultural Psychiatry to which he belongs.

Pierre Delion, 2017

CHAPTER ONE

Establishments and institutions

You write: "Institution in the sense of institutional psychotherapy: What care institutions are we going to create especially for this patient, here and now?"[2] Could you explain the concept of care institution in detail by showing me some examples of your way of treatment?

The word "institution" often has, in French, the meaning of a disproportionate and uncontrollable machine, on which one cannot act sufficiently for it to render the expected services. For example, people often say that national education, with its nearly two million civil servants, is an unmanageable institution, and that one should start by "trimming the fat" to be able to hope for change. But when Tosquelles introduces the distinction between establishment and institution, he decides to give the institution a

---

[2] P. Delion, *Mon combat …*, op. cit., p. 86.

dimension of humanization that the establishment does not have *a priori*. And he insists on the fact that if the establishment comes from the state to fulfill a specific mission (hospitals for care, high schools for education, museums for culture, etc.), the institution results from what the professionals charged by the establishment with fulfilling these missions do together.

For example, when the therapeutic club of a psychiatry department organizes a therapeutic activity, the latter is the result of meetings between patients and caregivers who have decided together to carry out the suggested activity, have voted a budget to achieve it, and have contacted resource people to make it work. In this case, the therapeutic club is an institution, in the sense that the patients and the caregivers rely together on its functioning, its rules, and its uses to end up creating the activity as desired by the patients and the caregivers involved. If the establishment's authorization had to be obtained, the response would take a long time to come and the form imposed by it would not correspond to what is expected, reinforcing the mechanisms of dependence and passivity of caregivers and patients.

But institutional psychotherapy (I.P.) proposes to go even further, by defining the transferential constellation as the most suitable form to treat each patient; the meeting of the constellation constitutes the institution closest to the problem of a patient. These institutions must include some characteristics that are essential for their optimal functioning: an opportunity to meet and talk together about the difficulties encountered in contact with the patient, an ability to adapt to changes that are bound to occur in the patient's care, and flexibility of operation, despite statutory constraints, which allows the spirit of initiative of the caregivers and the patient to be retained.

All this is to say that the current tendency to "protocolize" treatment (in the case of schizophrenia or autism, the protocol to be followed is defined by scientific circles in general) is in deep contradiction to the spirit of the institution in the sense of I.P. We could compare the protocols to the manufacture of "ready-to-wear costumes" as opposed to institutions inclined to manufacture "tailor-made costumes."

For instance, a child is followed on an outpatient basis for depression and intellectual inhibition. His psychotherapist sees him for a few months, then notices that there has been a worsening of the child's clinical condition due to the care being insufficient. The psychotherapist talks about it at the team meeting and suggests increasing the healing time for the child. The transferential constellation of the first months is concentrated in his psychotherapist, then, as other people join him, in the speech therapist, psychomotor therapist, educator, and so on. His transferential constellation unfolds and forms a small team that accompanies the child until his condition improves sufficiently to return to the initial individual psychotherapy. We are not locked in a binary logic such that the child's depression must be treated according to the protocol established by a review of the scientific literature, but, rather, we take up a logic of complexity, which implies that according to the clinical evolution of the child, his institution adapts to him and his psychopathology.

I.P. (institutional psychotherapy) therefore requires institutions that are distinct from establishments in order to bring the human environment to life in the most fruitful way possible, but these first-rate institutions (the therapeutic club, the meeting of patients with caregivers, the general assembly of the nursing staff, etc.) must help build second-order institutions (transferential constellations), centered on each patient. The subtle dialectic which must exist between the two orders rests in part on the human qualities of those who give them life, as opposed to the morbid and entropic processes which make them once again become asylum-seekers, and ultimately, die.

CHAPTER TWO

Active therapy

In the History of Institutional Psychotherapy, *Jean Oury often says that we must "treat the institution." How do you treat the institution?*

When François Tosquelles, condemned to death by Franco for his active participation in the Spanish Republican army (as head of the psychiatric service), had to flee his country and arrived in France in 1939, he took with him several psychiatry books that were dear to him. Among these works were Lacan's thesis devoted to a case of female paranoia (the Aimée case), already translated into Spanish, and a work by Hermann Simon, *Pour une thérapeutique plus active à l'hôpital psychiatrique*.[3] The latter, written in the 1930s by a psychoanalytically trained psychiatrist from Gütersloh,

---

[3] J. Lacan, *De la psychose paranoïaque dans ses rapports avec la personnalité* [1932], Paris: Seuil, 1980.

Germany, insists that in order for a psychiatric hospital to truly treat the mentally ill, it is absolutely necessary that it looks after itself. This means that those in charge of the establishment must take care of the caregivers so that they can properly care for the sick. In this book, Simon also stresses the importance of encouraging patients to practice various activities (manual, artistic, intellectual, social) to prevent them from falling into inactivity, which would increase their pathological apragmatism.

Tosquelles, to implement Simon's teaching, insists on the importance of distinguishing between establishment and institution. The establishment is, for example, the hospital in which the reception and care of the sick take place—but we all know that, depending on the professionals who work in this hospital, the results obtained will be extremely different: some will be satisfied with legal guidelines while others will show initiative and enthusiasm.

For Tosquelles, the institution is the "human tissue" that gives a hospital its "humanity." We know that in the field of psychiatry, the humanity of the psychiatric team is fundamental to the quality of patient care. Based on these premises, it is therefore necessary to "treat the institution," as Jean Oury proposed, in order to take into account the difficulties encountered when patients present with particular psychopathologies, such as serious mental illnesses.

So, what can we do to "treat the institution"? How can we take care of the people who embody and constitute the institution, that is to say, the professionals of different positions who make it up?

2.1 Insanity and social alienation

To answer this fundamental question, it is necessary to take a detour through the psychopathological specificities of serious mental illnesses, and in particular through what happens to the people who live in contact with them, both their families and their caregivers. In fact, if we do not take these specificities into consideration, patients will "trigger" the same alienating phenomena in their caring entourage as in their family and social surroundings at the onset of their illness.

Oury distinguishes two types of alienation: (1) mental or psychopathological alienation and (2) social alienation. The first is due to the effects induced by the mental illness itself which alienate the patient: he hears voices that others do not hear, he experiences extremely strong anxieties which destabilize him, or he acts without knowing why. In short, he suffers from serious symptoms that he cannot easily share with others and whose meaning, or potential meaning, escapes his understanding in most cases.

The second, social alienation, concerns the effects induced by the perception of the strangeness, on the part of the patient's entourage, of the symptoms of the patient, which results in the entourage moving away from him for fear of what could happen in contact with him. If a man walks down the street, restless and prey to bizarre gestures and behaviors, an ordinary citizen tends to move away from him, but this creates in the patient a feeling of rejection which contributes to social alienation.

2.2 Multireferential transference and dissociated transference

In mental alienation, psychopathologists, especially post-Kleinian psychoanalysts, have studied the transferential mechanisms that govern the patient's relationship with the world. But because they took essentially a perspective of individual psychoanalysis, they did not sufficiently take into consideration the specific form of transference in psychotic pathologies.

It was Tosquelles who, as one of the first to do so, proposed to characterize the transference of psychotic people by its multireferentiality (multireferential transference). For example, a patient arrives at the hospital to be treated because he presents an acute psychotic decompensation. He is greeted by a nurse with whom he feels listened to and safe. Then he is received by a psychiatrist with whom he does not feel at ease. Finally, the person who brings him his meal is immediately invested with closeness and care. With the nurse, he likes to talk and reveals a lot about his life. On the other hand, with the psychiatrist, he does not speak and refuses all confidence. As for the person in charge of the meal, he is familiar with her from the outset.

Tosquelles calls this patient's transferential relationship "multireferential": three people have met him, and each has shared a significantly different experience with him. Yet all three aspects are equally important; these three "referents" are invested with different or even antagonistic properties by the patient; together they are the transferential receptacle of this patient, his institution.

It is not a question of knowing who is right about him, but rather of finding out how to bring together these three experiences to better approach what the patient is going through, because these three experiences belong to the same patient. Tosquelles invents the "transferential constellation reunion," and in doing so he embodies the institution for the patient. Ultimately, it is a matter of creating a specific institution for each patient.

Later, Oury will refine the concept of multireferential transference to prefer that of "dissociated transference." Taking up from Bleuler (the inventor of the concept of schizophrenia) the dissociation at the origin of the schizophrenic process, Oury considers the person with schizophrenia to have a dissociated relationship with the world: his transference with caregivers will therefore also be dissociated. Tosquelles and Oury agree that the most specific form of institution for the patient is the transferential constellation and its reunion.

2.3 What is a transferential constellation?

These are all the people who are in contact with the patient. The reunion of the transferential constellation is the meeting instituted between these different people. In these meetings, everyone is called to speak about their experiences with the sick person, in all authenticity. Contradictory points of view are not the object of "rectifications" to find out who is right, but, on the contrary, the object is to find discrepancies between experiences that confirm the dissociation syndrome.

What counts in this operation is the ability to share different experiences within the institution without opposing them, thus producing a containment function for the patient, who cannot solve this problem on his own without the help of caregivers. In addition, by being able to talk about their experience, however bizarre, mad, or distressing, with a patient in the transferential constellation reunion, each caregiver transforms the "insane" elements that he (or she of course) received from the patient into something understandable, which helps him to find meaning for himself and for the patient in his professional work. Sometimes he finds an intellectual and emotional interest in these meetings, even a shared pleasure in "a job well done" with other caregivers. In doing so, we treat the institution, in the sense that the caregivers are encouraged to welcome, observe, understand what ordinary citizens consider "crazy," and thus to exercise their professional role of caregivers better.

2.4 Transferential constellations and organizational difficulties

On the other hand, many clinical examples show us that when caregivers cannot speak easily in the transferential constellation reunion, for many different reasons, the elements of experience that they cannot evoke will remain in them to act out negatively, contributing to the patient's alienation: both psychopathological alienation, which they shared with the patient in the transference, and social alienation, which they reconstitute to protect themselves from him. The effects then obtained are totally the opposite of the previous scenario. Each caregiver is no longer listened to, the institution is no longer "cared for," and therefore, quickly, it no longer treats the sick. It is therefore a matter of doing everything possible so that caregivers are deeply helped in their intellectual and emotional functions in order to be able to help patients come out of their alienation, allowing themselves to be cared for by the institution.

If we want to go further in explaining the psychopathological transferential mechanisms that are in question, we can distinguish two main types of transference in pre-oedipal psychopathology (psychosis, autism).

2.5 Projective identification and adhesive identification

In psychoses, the prevalent mechanism is "pathological projective identification." Discovered by Melanie Klein, it is described in her article on schizoid mechanisms of 1946, inspired by the work of Freud on the "projection" at the base of Schreber's delirium (1910).

Melanie Klein suggested that we adapt the concept of "projection" to the developing child, grappling with the identification mechanisms at work in all development: it is essentially a question of projecting, often unconsciously, in the other, the "bad objects" that one no longer wants to keep in oneself. As a result, if I throw at the other a bad object about the persecuting gaze, when I meet someone in the street, I can wonder why he looks at me in a hostile way, because I have projected in him the hostility that I no longer tolerated in me. I may have to attack him by saying, "Why are you looking at me like that, in a hostile way?" And it is easy to understand that the other person, brutally confronted with this question, not only does not understand it, but also experiences it as unbearable aggression. In this example, I have projected into the other a hostility that I no longer tolerated in myself, while the other did not initially hold any hostility towards me.

The world can quickly become persecutory. I want to make it clear that these mechanisms can exist in normal life—as long as we do not remain in a state of conviction. It often happens that we attribute our misfortunes to others; but a wake-up call allows things to be quickly put back in place, and the ease that made us attribute our own difficulties to others immediately resolves itself. With psychotic people, these beliefs are absolutely not undermined by this reality check. And if we transpose this situation from everyday life to that of professionals in psychiatry, we immediately see that what can be endured by everyone as an exception cannot be endured repeatedly every day, several times per day, in coexistence with the sick.

Caregivers must therefore be helped to receive in a welcoming manner these projection elements (which I propose to call "projectiles") which invade their daily life, but also to transform them so as not to be "filled up" with all these "projectiles," and ultimately end up with two possibilities: either "burnout" syndrome, when they continue to want to accommodate the symptoms of the sick, or the "armored" syndrome, when they form a defensive shell that protects them from projectiles, but which, at the same time, also keeps them away from their caring duties.

In autism, the prevalent mechanism is "adhesive identification." This mechanism was discovered by Esther Bick in 1967 in the form of "adhesive identity"[4] and was taken up by Donald Meltzer in 1975. In its development, the baby goes through a phase

---

[4] E. Bick, "L'expérience de la peau dans les relations précoces" [1967], in *Les écrits de Martha Harris et d'Esther Bick*, Larmor Plage: Éditions du Hublot, 1998.

in which everything happens as if its representations were reduced to a world of surfaces, a two-dimensional universe. Clinging to a sensation is then the defense available to him when his continuity of existence is threatened. After a few weeks of development, the baby begins to search for what is behind surfaces. He enters a new three-dimensional world, whose depth opens the world of surfaces onto that of volumes. In this new world, projective identification becomes possible.

Here is a clinical example: A child with autism tries to move from one room to the other, but he invariably stops in the doorway. He does a flapping with both hands, and, seeing me, grabs me to step into the other room. The type of transference this child makes with me is adhesive. He shows me that he has remained in a world in which anxieties are fundamental: constantly falling, bursting into pieces, liquefying. The caregivers who work with autistic children usually have marks on their bodies from these pathological latchings-on.

These symptoms are less intrusive than those described for psychosis but are no less worrying. Caregivers of autistic children must also be present at reunions of transferential constellations, in which talking about the experiences with the autistic children in question is crucial for understanding their psychopathology.

So, if we go back to the question from the beginning "How to treat the institution?" and if we recognize the institution as all the people who "revolve" around patients while remaining alive with them, we see that it is a question of allowing caregivers to welcome patients in good conditions, to observe the transference phenomena that they establish with them by using the transferential constellations in depth—so that their human capacities of reception are protected and allow them to better understand patients' psychopathology. Thus, the caregivers of the institution can help patients in an appropriate way to resolve their basic anxieties.

Supporting caregivers is therefore essential so that they in turn can support patients: This is what I call "phoric function." As parents must carry their babies for development until they can support themselves on their legs and in their mind, in the same way, caregivers must "carry" patients on their "psychic shoulders," to take care of them, during all the time necessary for them to achieve sufficient autonomy.

Caring for the institution is therefore a necessary prerequisite for any possible treatment of mental illness.

CHAPTER THREE

Institutional psychotherapy and antipsychiatry

Could you explain to me in detail your memories of your first meeting with Oury at La Borde and about the meeting with Cooper at Guattari's? In your opinion, is Guattari a supporter of antipsychiatry?

When I first met Jean Oury, it was a Sunday in the summer of 1976 at La Borde. One of the doctors at my Angers hospital, Jean Colmin, author of an interesting book on the location of his team in the geodemographic sector under his responsibility, had organized a meeting with Oury at La Borde, with the participation of several of my colleagues from Angers (Henry, Denis, Le Roux, Mercier). Along with Oury, Félix Guattari, Danielle Roulot, and Brivette Buchanan were present.

Oury's office is an extraordinary place, filled with books and stories. We talked about the situation at our hospital and our idea of meeting regularly with him and others to support, together, a strategy for a change in the Central and West psychiatric departments. It was the time of the establishment of the sector (1973–1974), and the developments of each service were interesting to analyze together. We then agreed to a quarterly meeting in an old chateau-restaurant near Angers on Sunday, the only day available for most of us. The de Brignac group began its meetings in November 1976, and Oury attended until his death in 2014. We covered a lot of the themes of the institution, and it helped each of the participants to work toward an interesting development in his service, and in his hospital.

At the same time as these meetings, I went many times to La Borde to meet Oury and work with him, either for supervisions of complex clinical cases, or to discuss specific theoretical and clinical points. One of the first meetings took place with a schizophrenic patient that I referred to him at La Borde. During this joint consultation, I witnessed a great clinical lesson that fundamentally changed my way of understanding the function of meetings. The patient seemed very distressed when the end of the consultation was about to happen. Oury had noticed that the patient was looking at his hand and forearm resting on his desk with great concern, and in a comment that was both light and precise, he reassured him by saying, "Don't worry, your hand won't stay on my desk, it will remain with you." The patient got up and left us, reassured, after greeting us both. What a lesson in body image dissociation and what you can do with it!

Later, at the end of 1978, Oury called Tosquelles on the phone with me being present, so that I could go and do an internship in his service at La Candélie, in Agen. And there, I met the founder of I.P., and I spent my entire internship in consultation with him and the patients in his department. This new meeting confirmed Oury's lesson: the institution is secondary to the meeting with the patient. Only his transferential psychopathology can guide us in the construction with him of his adequate institution.

As for the meeting with Guattari, as early as 1976, with Oury, the story is not the same. At the time, I was still a little seduced by certain theories of antipsychiatry, in particular about the importance of the quality of the reception of patients deemed to be alienated as well as by the idea of not systematically hospitalizing them. Guattari was not strictly speaking a follower of antipsychiatry, for he was anything but naïve! But, on the other hand, he was eminently interested in politics, and as such, he was in contact with all progressive forces, including Italian and English antipsychiatrists in particular, but also with many avant-garde groups around the world. I had asked him if I might participate in the meetings he was organizing on this topic and, sensing my interest in these subjects that fascinated him, he invited me to come to his home, rue de Condé, in Paris.

This is how I met a number of well-known and lesser-known people, including David Cooper. Unfortunately, Cooper had become a "star" of antipsychiatry, and the publication of his books by *Éditions du Seuil*, from 1972, corresponded to the moment when he had left England to come to live in France. In France, his positions garnered a certain interest from Guattari and Maud Mannoni. And while his English practice was worth being known and appreciated, like those of Laing, Esterson, and Berke, his transition from practitioner to writer took him away from clinical reality: his message became much less alive, and mostly ideological. We sympathized nonetheless, and when I was commissioned to edit an issue of *Psychiatric Care* on schizophrenia, he agreed to write an article for nurses summarizing his point of view. And then he passed away too soon: born in 1931, he died in 1986 in Paris. All these people, even if I have not always been in perfect agreement with them (in particular with Cooper), contributed to my formation in a decisive way, and I pay them a strong tribute for what they have given to me.

CHAPTER FOUR

Transversality and institutional analysis

Could you give me your opinion on the concept of institutional analysis and that of transversality?

Institutional analysis is a concept that was invented by Hélène Chaigneau, a great friend of Oury. She distinguishes analysis from psychoanalysis: institutional analysis focuses on the analysis that I.P. actors must constantly make of what is happening in the community concerned and, in its environment, of the balance of power between the various administrative, bureaucratic, and nursing components, in order to draw up an overall strategy aimed at allowing the institution to function in as harmonious a manner as possible.

For example, in the hospital and sector service in which I work, it is very important to know the perspective of the administrative director of psychiatry *vis-à-vis* a project that we are implementing; because if he is in favor of it, he will directly help us to achieve it, while if he is not, he will set up blocks (conscious or unconscious), and we will not be able to achieve it. And in day-to-day care, it can happen that a significant resistance is the result of a few nurses influenced by a trade union movement hostile to I.P. Sometimes, it is the doctors in the service who are caught up in another ideology, such as antipsychiatry or the prevalence of genetics and neurosciences, and whether consciously or not, they will prevent the service from moving toward a better I.P. practice. The institutional analysis allows for a permanent checkup on the "state of the troops," and on what is available for engagement. This analysis is often done in a group of motivated people interested in a profound change in the service, in the direction of I.P.

Transversality is a concept that was invented by Guattari to explain the difference between the statutory hierarchy (the director is above the doctor who is above the nurses) and the hierarchy that I propose to call "subjective," the one that Oury calls for when he says that he is for an absolute hierarchy (each caregiver is different from the others and his skills go well beyond his diplomas). Transversality tries to take into account the transfer which cannot be deployed in an organization based solely on the statutory hierarchy. An example is that of the cook, Janine, who is invested by an autistic child when he does not want to go to see the psychiatrist, or the psychologist, or the teacher. This is because of the transversal relationship between the doctor in charge and Janine, who does not have a place as a caregiver in the statutory hierarchy, but for whom I have esteem because she knows how to welcome children very seriously affected, that she will be able to come to constellation meetings and help us care for this autistic child. Therefore, the transfer is compatible with transversality, while it is not within the statutory hierarchy.

From my point of view—and I thank you for having spotted them—these two concepts of institutional analysis and transversality are very important for the ordinary functioning of I.P.

For my part, I very often organized strategy meetings in the services in which I worked in order to carry out an institutional analysis with a few trusted people who were not interested in power relations, but rather in the quality of the work accomplished. And often, in these meetings of caregivers of different professional status, the question of transversality arose. My experience has shown me that the head of department or the manager must take a step toward others in order to open the process of transversality, which cannot easily come from people who are located "at the bottom" of the statutory hierarchy. And yet, it is by involving all concerned in the meetings of the transferential constellations that they become effective.

CHAPTER FIVE

The welcoming function

You write: "The institution is first of all in the mind of the one who receives the child first, then, as and when the meetings are organized with and around him, it is made up of the people that he or she will more or less invest, positively or negatively."[5] Could we then say that the first phase of the institution is the transfer or the emotion on the part of the staff for the patients?

When we receive a child in consultation with his parents, we try to welcome them in such a way that they feel recognized in their psychic suffering, and relieved to have met us. This is the question often put forward by Oury of the reception function. But this reception should also make it possible to resolve the question of diagnosing the child's pathology. Once this first step has been carried out, and if the diagnosis requires it, for example for an

---

[5] P. Delion, *Mon combat ...*, op. cit., p. 95.

autistic child, we offer to welcome him in a day hospital to observe him (in the sense of observation according to Esther Bick) and to build the "tailor-made" institution that suits him. In this arrangement, we can begin to see how the child is in the world, how he does within the institutional framework offered to him. From this point of view, the child invests the arrangement (the material framework and the caregivers) with what we call the transference to his environment. And that triggers emotions, affects, or what we call a countertransference, in the caregivers. The work then consists of receiving, carrying within, and understanding what comes from the child, but also the effects of what comes from the child on the caregivers who accompany him. For that, we need a logical triad that I propose to formulate by the phoric, semaphoric, and metaphoric functions.

The phoric function (*pherein* means "to carry" in ancient Greek) is the arrangement that caregivers use to "carry" (in the sense of Winnicott's *holding*) the child as long as is necessary. "Carrying" is an allusion to the carrying of babies by their parents, not only in their surrounding arms, but also in their psychic attention. The caregivers welcome and provide psychic attention to the autistic child who arrives at the day hospital. In doing so, they place their own psychic apparatus at the disposal of the child and, as a result, they receive all the signs that come from the child and which reflect his anxieties, his appeasements, his questions. By being available to the child, the caregivers exercise a "semaphoric function" (*sema* = sign; therefore, "bearers of signs"). They are the receptacles of the signs of psychic suffering of the child; in other words, they can describe the signs presented by the child, but often they cannot understand the meaning at first.

For example, an autistic child suddenly throws himself at me when I arrive at the day hospital. He hooks his hand around my neck and hurts me badly. His gaze avoids me, and the more I try to remove his hand from my neck because it hurts so badly, the more the child digs his fingernails into my skin.

I am the bearer of the child's signs (semaphore function), but I do not understand why he does this. These clinical findings need to be recounted in the transferential constellation meeting where I meet my colleagues. In this meeting, another caregiver then shares his experience at the same time, then a third caregiver says that he understands that the child only behaves this way if he is surprised to see us arrive at an unusual moment. When this happened to him, he sang the nursery rhyme that reassures the child at the end of the Conte workshop, and the child then agreed to spontaneously let go of the caregiver's neck.

The sharing of experiences between the caregivers is an exchange of the countertransference of each of them, and what did not make sense for the first one has some meaning for all those who participate in the meeting of the constellation: it is the "metaphorical function" (access to meaning). It is not about "interpreting" for the child what the caregivers have understood, but it changes the way the caregivers are with the child after the meeting.

If a similar experience arises, the caregivers will understand that this child, when he sees a professional arrive at an unusual time of day, is suddenly invaded by archaic anxieties related to the "sameness" that structures him. Various strategies are then possible to help him get out of the deadlock he is getting into and allow the people who take care of him to do so. A sign that didn't seem to make any sense is attributed some meaning thanks to the "transferential constellation" in the institution.

CHAPTER SIX

Continuity of care

*F*or Tosquelles and Oury, patient flow and continuity of care are fundamental. In Angers, then in Lille, you tried to invent the circulation of patients and the continuity of care with the people of the Fine Arts. How did you maintain the de-completeness[6] ratios or the institutional flexibility?

Patient circulation involves the spatiality of the arrangement, while the continuity of care emphasizes temporality. Continuity of care was the basis for the creation of sector psychiatry, since it gave caregivers the possibility of supporting patients over the long term, as long as necessary.

We know that mental illnesses such as autism or schizophrenia are not transient illnesses, but usually last a lifetime. But if sector psychiatry makes it possible to follow patients for all the time

---

[6] P. Delion, *Mon combat …*, op. cit., p. 106.

necessary, they still need to have the freedom to move around in the spaces in which they can invest what they wish, without encountering limitations. Restrictions prevent the expression of their desire, and this in respect of the law, in general. It is not about making emergency laws for the mentally ill that would remove them from the ordinary world.

The freedom of movement of patients therefore becomes a condition for the possibility of their care, in order to help them build a spatio-temporal tabulation of their world: I go to see my psychiatrist in his office at such and such an hour; then, I will go to the workshop where I continue to build a piece of furniture with the workshop instructor. Then I will go to the therapy club meeting where we are to discuss the stay organized this summer. If I'm in good shape, then I'll go have tea in the cafeteria, and head back to my lodging to rest a bit, before watching the evening movie on television.

For this organization planned by the patient, it is absolutely necessary that the doors be open, that the spaces be accessible, that the caregivers be available. Indeed, if on entering the workshop the patient discovers that one of his persecutors is present, it is important that he cannot go there without being the object of some reprimand. In short, if we want free movement to work in a place of care, this requires careful thought by caregivers on the organization of the system. But when it "works," the patient will be able to choose the trajectory he wants in all the institutions offered. As a result, each patient uses a few available spaces (manual, cultural, sports, group activities, etc.) which constitute for him the elements of his "tailor-made institution."

These elements can be found in the hospital ward, but also outside the hospital. All must be thought of in "complementary relationships" so that the patient feels that he is the common subject of all these treatments rather than the object of control of each of the caregivers. And in order not to move toward a totalizing, if not totalitarian, system, I proposed, with Oury, to call "de-completeness relations" the links that characterize the reunion of the different people invested by the patient. The transferential constellation is therefore governed by relations of de-completeness.

This is the *raison d'être* of I.P.: to organize the institutions so that they are accessible in free circulation (spatiality) and according to a logic of de-completeness relations, and for all the time that will be necessary (temporality). This leads me to say that sector psychiatry is the administrative organization proposed by law for the functioning of psychiatry in France, while institutional psychotherapy is its method.

In this perspective, we have developed a certain number of collaborations with partners in the city who help us by welcoming children for various activities, and in particular cultural activities.

In Lille, for example, we have developed activities with those in charge of Fine Arts aimed at promoting, on the one hand, the reception of autistic children, and on the other hand, in-depth work on violence with children and adolescents from disadvantaged neighborhoods.

For the first, it was a question of allowing autistic children to benefit through their classes of working sessions in the Museum of Fine Arts. These activities take place once a week and focus on drawing and painting, then include the possibility of creating short animated films produced in a collaboration. Children with autism can come accompanied by a parent to help them share their cultural activities with their families. This often allows children in the class who are not autistic to discover in their classmate that autism, while it makes social relations difficult, does not prevent them from having talents that this unusual context allows them to explore. Exhibition of works at the end of the school year is often an opportunity to highlight the value of integrating such different children, when possible, into an ordinary environment.

For the second, the approach is appreciably different, since it involves getting adolescents to discover violence through classic paintings, often mythological, and to understand the age of their creation. Different media are then used to express inspiration by these works, in order to transform the adolescents into actors of new discovery: imitating the painting in a group, drawing the structure of the painting, imagining a scenario preceding the painting of the painting, writing about the painting, and so on. A professional photographer accompanies the group during the school year and regularly returns the shots of the adventure. An exhibition of the paintings studied takes place at the end of the year, and the teenagers are transformed for the occasion into guides for their parents and teachers. The experiments carried out over several years show an appropriation of the concepts governing violence, a reasoned criticism of the effects of violence, an improvement of the team spirit in the classes concerned, and finally, an increase of the intellectual appetite for academic knowledge.

These experiments carried out by partners outside the healthcare sector illustrate the functioning of de-completeness reports. Indeed, cultural organizers, parents, teachers, the directors of the Fine Arts are called upon to give their testimonies on these unusual experiences, and their opinions, resolutely decoupled from those of the caregivers, are always interesting to take into consideration in the transferential constellation.

Obviously, all this work does not take place with a snap of the fingers: it is the consequence of a long process of collaboration with the elected officials of the town hall, and especially of a request made to me by Martine Aubry (mayor of Lille) to help him think about the phenomenon of violence in his city.

CHAPTER SEVEN

The flesh, the thing

*I*n Lille, against scientism, you teach institutional psychotherapy at the university with the complementary points of view of anthropology of medicine (Lévi-Strauss) and psychopathology (Oury, Tosquelles). So how do you deal with the distinction between the thing and the flesh? This is an essential point of institutional psychotherapy.

For the film directed by Nicolas Philibert on La Borde, the title that was chosen was *La moindre des choses*.[7] Oury often said that his job was to organize a welcoming and efficient psychiatry for all patients, and especially for psychotic people. And he would add, "That's the least of it, isn't it?" So, for him, "institutional psychotherapy is psychiatry," which means that institutional

---

[7] Cf. N. Philibert, *La moindre des choses* followed by *The invisible*, Les films d'ici/La sept cinéma, 1996, Éditions Montparnasse.

psychotherapy is a modality of practice of psychiatry that puts the subject first. But when he spoke of the "thing," Oury often referred his listeners to reading Freud about the "thing representation" of the object (as opposed to the "word representation" of the object), and to variations of Lacan on "*das Ding*."

For Oury, the thing is essential in so far as each of us invests things according to our family and personal history, and these things become "presences" beside us that go far beyond their material and economic aspects. These things are invested by the subject and have places and functions sometimes crucial in the trajectory of the person.

For patients, things can be of considerable importance depending on each person's history, and it happens that during random encounters, about which Oury has also said and written a lot ("Programming the Random"), some things can resurface in contact with one another, and sometimes with very important results.

In such situations, we can therefore say that the subject of flesh has projected into the thing a libidinal investment which makes it alive in his eyes, and often witness to "something" of his history. So, the flesh and the thing are not opposed, but in a relation of contingency: for such and such a subject of flesh, such and such a thing has such and such a meaning.

From this perspective, "the least of things" is the hope that something can serve as support for the subject, confirming the phoric function for which any institution worthy of the name is responsible. And in such a perspective, the thing can become "animated" and generate an animist vision of the world: even if Westerners deny themselves to be animists, their vision of the world is permanently caught up in this transferential movement with things of the surrounding world.

CHAPTER EIGHT

Deinstitutionalize?

*I*n Lille, there is an insistent movement of de-hospitalization, or rather of "de-establishment," with the mobile sector team.[8] In this movement, we insist on the concept of deinstitutionalization. Can we say that institutional psychotherapy in the psychiatric hospital and the mobile sector team are both necessary as the ideal image of psychiatry?

In Lille, there is indeed a powerful movement, that of deinstitutionalization. It is taken forward in particular by Jean-Luc Roelandt who leads an extremely energetic and efficient policy of psychiatry in the city. If I share with him the great interest of delivering this work in depth in and with the city, I think, on the other hand, that the disenchantment with the hospital, under the

---

[8] Cf. P. Delion, *Accueillir et soigner la souffrance psychique de la personne*, Paris: Albin Michel, 2013, p. 123.

pretext that it increases the alienation of patients, is a received idea of the antipsychiatry viewpoint that has not been sufficiently considered in the light of institutional psychotherapy.

Rather than pleading for the elimination of mental hospitals, I really believe that we must work to transform them to make them welcoming and human. Indeed, it happens in most cases that during a lifetime of an autistic or schizophrenic patient, or for other psychiatric pathologies, recourse to hospitalization is necessary *on the condition* that this hospitalization is carried out in a welcoming and human service, that it be organized in continuity with the previous follow-up and with the subsequent follow-up, and that the caregivers who accompany the patient are as far as possible the same: this obligatory passage can become a very structuring step in the overall care of the patient.

If there is a mobile team for me, it is the team in the sector in which the patient lives. Making the mobile team a concept separate from the practice of the sector is, in my opinion, a fetishization of the specificities of the functions of caregivers which ultimately goes against an organization by which the follow-up of the patient is carried out by the same caregivers throughout his care.

Today, a number of psychiatrists have isolated with their mobile team a group of caregivers who are specialized in this single function. In doing so, the importance is placed on the intervention at home, or in any other place favorable to a meeting with the patient, but under the primacy of emergency and crisis. However, crisis finds, by definition, the right answers in what can be organized before and after in a logic of continuity that the crisis has disorganized.

Thinking that part of the sector team can specialize in these interventions shifts the center of gravity toward a logic of emergency care at the expense of that of continuity of care, the foundation of transferential sector psychiatry. For my part, I continue to teach and advocate a sector psychiatry faithful to its original doctrine, enlightened by the methods of I.P.

CHAPTER NINE

Sector psychiatry

How did the integration between sector psychiatry and I.P. take place in Angers, Reims, Landerneau, or Abbeville? Is the art activity usable in all places?

In Angers, when sector psychiatry was established, it was part of a working philosophy centered on institutional psychotherapy concerning the entire process of change. Integration was constitutive of the movement engaged. It was a question, following the recommendations of Bonnafé, of not showing up in the city saying, "What can I do for you?" without profoundly transforming the service by which the promises made to the sector would be fulfilled.

There is no question, in fact, of welcoming into the asylum hospitalization service a patient to whom one would have said that psychiatry was becoming more human. So, it was necessary to keep the two aspects together: radically change the hospital to humanize it, and install in the estate a sector psychiatry welcoming and available to patients.

For example, the modalities of forced hospitalization changed when we were able, with the mayors of the towns of the sector, to modify the previous conditions. Previously, the mayor was called for a psychiatric emergency: he took a psychiatric placement order, confirmed by the prefecture. From the installation of the sector, we were together at the homes of the patients and we were able to learn that the hospitalizations were done without recourse to coercion. Our practices with the population and our relations with elected municipal officials have been radically transformed in the direction of a humanization facilitating the establishment of sector psychiatry and I.P.

The experiences of Landerneau, Reims, and Abbeville, for example, followed parallel paths, different in their accomplishment, but inspired by the same organizing principles. In all cases, relations with culture (arts, cinema, theater, music, choir, exhibitions, *art brut*, etc.) have been more or less developed, depending on local resources, and have provided support for the teams of sector psychiatry seeking to register their activities in the city.

CHAPTER TEN

Work and adaptation

You wrote: "The institution can be in the city." I agree with you. But what should we pay attention to so as not to leave the patient in an isolated situation? For example, Tosquelles and Le Guillant debated this point. They argued over "bogus work." So, it would be "real work"—or, what does the institution do in the city?

I often stress the importance of words: it is not just about "going into the city," but, above all, "being with the city and its citizens." Indeed, there have been many experiences of renting apartments to accommodate patients who have spent many years in a psychiatric hospital. In the event that these patients were not sufficiently supported to create links with their neighbors, their social partners, their local professionals, their isolation has led to tragedies (suicides, decompensations, emergency re-hospitalizations, violence, etc.). Living with the city is the object of a work of integration into the social bonds of the district or the village, and therefore of a taming of the networks in question.

It is for this reason that we have created out-of-hospital therapeutic clubs, so as to offer a welcoming base of associations for patients followed on an outpatient basis, and thus help them to live in and with the city. After many years of operation, the teams of Angers, Landerneau, Reims, Abbeville, and others have thus been able to forge links with other associations, with municipalities, with sports clubs and cultural associations, allowing patients to find, according to their centers of interest, people with whom to develop social relations. Our experience has shown us that these methods are the best means of fighting the isolation which is the main effect of social alienation on every patient. It is therefore a question of combining this "social" support for the loneliness and isolation of patients with a real psychiatric follow-up carried out by the caregivers of each one's constellation.

Regarding the debate between Tosquelles and Le Guillant on therapeutic work, this is an historical misunderstanding, as Tosquelles advocated therapeutic work (akin to play) at the psychiatric hospital from before the establishment of the sector, to give each patient an activity fighting against asylum entropy and his own apragmatism, while Le Guillant derided this work, calling it "false work,"[9] and opposing it to the real work that the patient could find once the psychiatric decompensation was overcome.

For Tosquelles, in fact, "human destiny is not to adapt or perish, but to build with other men a world in which to 'become man.'" It is in this spirit that he attaches particular importance to two specifically human functions which are, on the one hand, language as a means of addressing the other and of sustaining one's own existence; and on the other hand, work as social organization, division

---

[9] Cf. "Symposium sur la psychothérapie collective. Bonneval, 9 Sept. 1952." in *Évolution psychiatrique*, vol. 3, 1952, pp. 531–532.

of tasks, a system of exchange. Based on these presuppositions, he believes that the therapeutic and restructuring function of work is essentially based on the part of initiation and activity that the patient can bring to it;[10] in doing so, he insists on the subjective mobilization underlying the action, with the realization of the subject in mind.

For Tosquelles, re-socialization through work wins out over vocational rehabilitation. Le Guillant is only interested in social and professional rehabilitation if the psychiatrist multiplies his efforts to transform the living environment and working conditions with which the patient will have to reconnect. He is more of an occupational psychiatrist (in the sense of occupational medicine) located in the world of workers to modify society, radically, according to the communist project.

If this debate could take place in the years 1950–1970, it is because of the possibility of finding work at that time, even with a status of mental patient. Today, most patients are declared "chronically disabled," receiving a "disabled adult allowance," and very few of them can benefit from a job, except to be employed in protected jobs. The opposition between real work and false work is therefore no longer really relevant.

---

[10] Cf. I. Billiard, *"Les pères fondateurs de la psychopathologie du travail en butte à l'énigme du travail"*, in *Cliniques méditerranéennes*, 66, 2002/2.

THE REPUBLIC
OF FALSE SELVES

Pierre Delion

Original publication details

La République des faux-selfs by Pierre Delion

Printed in France, at the ISIPRINT printing plant (Saint-Denis) in October 2018 on eco-responsible paper

Legal deposit: October 2018

© Éditions d'une, Paris, 2018

All reproduction, translation and adaptation rights reserved for all countries.

This edition translated and reproduced with the kind permission of the publisher.

*"A war against humanity's inter-relational practices
has been declared."*

*"Psychiatry, with pedagogy, education, justice, and social work,
is at the front line of this fight."*

Contents

Preface   55

1. Politics   57

2. Media, opinions, images   65

3. But what is a false self?   69

4. Societal changes in relation to the inflation of the image   75

5. Discomfort in the helping relationship   79

6. Is there still a subject in man?   83

7. The psychiatric revolution   87

8. Sector psychiatry and institutional psychotherapy   93

9. Medicine with a human face   101

10. Human psychiatry   105

11. By way of conclusion   109

Preface

For several decades, we have lived in a world whose meaning escapes us more and more. This in spite of the democratic project which, at least in its beginning, prioritized meaningful social bonds as fundamental to its sustainment and cultivation.

It is precisely this state of (post-)democracy, threatened by neglect, that I propose to call "the republic of false selves" in order to describe the now dominant tendency to consider the impression the subject gives of himself (self/ego/me) as more important than his authentic self.

This phenomenon has considerable deleterious effects, which must be understood if we are to transform them into creative possibilities, thereby "restoring the subject within the individual."[11]

---

[11] See Jean Oury, *Le Collectif, Seminar 1985–1986*, Paris: Scarabée, 1986, re-ed. Nîmes: Champ Social, 2005.

It goes to the very heart of the work of all *psychistes*: pedagogues, educators, caregivers, judges, and all other professionals engaged with human relations.

And via the (ever more numerous) warnings of professionals of care, education, and justice at the front lines of attack on the subject-citizen, we see that democracy is now more radically a question of keeping alive the possibility of mutually constituting ourselves as free beings, even if only impermanently.

This book modestly attempts to examine the details of this complex situation, in order to return meaning to today's (political, medical, educational) practices, deprived of their own analytical tools in favor of techno-bureaucratic protocols and innovations, increasingly globalizing but also dehumanizing our societal bonds (*liens sociétaux*) at an alarming speed.

It is addressed to professionals who wish to resist this disintegrative tendency, even as it grows each day in strength, which is to say: to take up an ethical and courageous position and no longer to accept a kind of normative vagrancy justified solely by managerial logic.

Perhaps it will be of help, as a consequence, to those concerned with work in human relationships: to patients, to children, to dependent persons, to struggling citizens for whom we have become, in our defending body, the advocates for their defense in humanity.

No matter the cost, we must no longer remain silent in the face of this attack on all that binds together our singularities; we must leave behind consternation, and we must do so together to give life once again to the concept of a "collective," today drowned in the sands of an extreme individualism. We must also, each of us, reflect on the political arrangements that govern our ordinary life, whatever one may think of it—and especially when we ignore it.

CHAPTER ONE

Politics

The very idea of psychotherapy, whether individual or institutional, can find both the anchoring and the breathing-room it needs only in a democratic political system.
The freedom of movement of people, speech, and thought do not exist in a totalitarian system, or in a hidden, temporary, and therefore vulnerable way. On the contrary, psychotherapeutic work is based on the freedom of the circulation of thoughts in the minds of those who practice psychotherapy and of those who wish to benefit from it, as well as on the solidity of the contract which binds people around such a project. Free association, the cardinal rule of psychoanalysis, is one of the foundations of the psychotherapeutic contract. The free circulation of speech in the transferential constellation (as it was created and theorized in the institutional psychotherapy movement) is another example,

no less crucial for its contractual functioning. Indeed, the contract takes place between free and enlightened people and can only work if these elements are respected. In a totalitarian society, there is no possible contract except for leonine contracts or diktats.

Against these potential abuses, democracy guarantees the ability to resort to the law. But when democratic functioning is called into question, or when it becomes problematic to the point that some speak of "post-democracy,"[12] all the institutions that are essential to its maintenance, including the justice system and those that provide what we call "public services," are in jeopardy.

The institutions of democracy make it possible to meet the needs of the population as a people, a group of people governed by politics, by common decisions which institute a form of justice between citizens instead of the law of the strongest, or the cruelest, or the better off: to learn, to be cared for, to be informed, to be defended, to be free to associate with others, to believe or not, to have recourse to the law, to have a home, to accept differences, and so on, are all occurrences of it. But these inventions of democratic society can only be perpetuated if political functioning remains rational and neutral.

Too many politicians have let themselves be seduced by wealth, power, privilege, tolerance. In a democracy, the position of representative of the people might give politicians the idea that they are entitled to the privileges rendered to them; but history teaches us that it is precisely those who abuse their rights as citizens who discredit their representative functions the most, and largely contribute to tarnishing the image that their fellows have of politics. The recent Cahuzac case, where the finance minister in charge of combating tax fraud was himself guilty of it and jailed, is paradigmatic in this respect. Faced with such deplorable recent examples,

---

[12] Colin Crouch, *Post Democracy* (2004), trans. *Post-démocratie,* Paris: Diaphanes, 2013.

however, there are earlier interesting references, before the establishment of any democratic system.

According to tradition, Cincinnatus (519–430 BCE) was devoted to the cultivation of his lands when the senators came to beg him to agree to free the consul of Rome, taken hostage by the Aequi, in order to resolve the impending political crisis. Cincinnatus knew that his departure risked ruining his family, already impoverished following the trial of his son, the victim of a slander plotted by a rival, Marcus Volscius Fictor, if, in his absence, the crops were not insured. Nonetheless, he agreed. In sixteen days, he freed the besieged consul, defeated the Aequi at the battle of Mount Algid, celebrated a triumph in Rome, had Fictor condemned for false testimony towards his son, *and* resigned, returning to cultivate his field. His giving back of power at the end of the crisis then became, for Roman politicians, an example of good leadership, dedication to the public good, virtue, and modesty.[13]

But while democracy has been able to gain substance by relying on such examples, it has taken centuries for it to emerge from its long history of successive political regimes. Montesquieu taught us that the democratic system is based on the existence and separation of the three (executive, legislative, and judicial) powers. It now appears that a fourth power, that of the media, is necessary for the information of the free persons who together form the people of democracy. For Abraham Lincoln, democracy was "government of the people, by the people, for the people." This definition is close to the etymological meaning of the term "democracy": the power (*kratos*) of/to the people (*demos*). It is repeated in the Preamble to the 1958 Constitution of the Fifth French Republic.

---

[13] Sextus Aurelius Victor, *Hommes illustres de la ville de Rome*, XVII, L "Quinctius Cincinnatus," in *Œuvres complètes*, translation and comments by André Dubois and Yves Germain, Clermont-Ferrand: Paléo, 2003.

However, this definition remains susceptible to different interpretations, both as regards the concrete meaning of popular sovereignty and in its practical application, which appears clearly in the light of the diversity of political regimes that have claimed and claim to be based on the model of democracy.

Generally speaking, and from a historical point of view, a government is said to be "democratic" as opposed to "monarchical" (where power is held by one), or "oligarchic" (where power is held by a small group of individuals). These oppositions, inherited from Greek philosophy, are now nuanced by the existence of parliamentary monarchies. More recently, Karl Popper defined democracy as opposed to "dictatorship,"[14] considering that it allows the people to control their rulers, and to oust them in an established way without resorting to a revolution.[15]

Thus, the term "democracy" does not refer only to forms of government, but also to a society based on freedom and equality (see, e.g., Tocqueville[16]), or more generally still, to a set of values: political, social, or cultural ideals and principles.

A democratic society can, in theory, function either directly or indirectly, depending on whether it opts for a system of representation of the people or not. At the time when he wrote *Du contrat social* (1762), Jean-Jacques Rousseau claimed that democracy could only be direct: "Sovereignty cannot be represented, for the same reason that it cannot be alienated; it consists essentially in the general will and the general will is not represented."[17]

---

[14] Karl Popper, *La Leçon de ce siècle* (1993), re-ed. Paris, 10/18, 1997.
[15] Today, we see the political maneuvers of several leaders of large countries go well beyond this basic democratic functioning, in particular: Russia, Turkey, and China.
[16] Alexis de Tocqueville, De la démocratie en Amérique: Souvenirs, L'Ancien Régime et la Révolution (1832), re-ed. Paris: Robert Laffont, coll. *"Bouquins"*, 1986.
[17] Jean-Jacques Rousseau, *Du contrat social* (1762), III, 15, re-ed. Paris: Flammarion, 2001.

But our contemporary societies, faced with the theoretical and practical difficulties of such an operation, have chosen the second system and are now evolving in the mode of representative democracies. Now voters have to choose candidates to represent them.

However, the communication strategies of candidates for political affairs have become more and more efficient, using oral, written, broadcast, and digital media. We are here very far from the oratorical oppositions of the ancient Greeks: in terms of argumentation, we come rather to an impoverishment of language in favor of a functional (even behaviorist) "efficiency" of language in a way that evokes the "banality of evil" (thoughtlessness) of which Hannah Arendt speaks: the disempowerment of the acting subject, and the denial of any critical thought, however little enlightened.

Under these conditions, following the *management* model which currently predominates (i.e., in terms of "rapidity of amortization" and "securing of the resources invested" with regard to "psychosocial risks"), it is much safer to take advantage of the fact that quantitatively, we have never "communicated" so much to dilute the political in the *doxa* and to see ourselves "elected" (and let us not spoil our joy, all the more envied that the merit is less) by virtue of mediocrity!

A number of techniques of lobbying the powerful and/or manipulating citizens through images resulting from techniques of suggestion based on knowledge of the mechanisms of control, and largely dependent on the sums collected for these purposes, have been considerably developed, and have come to mar democratic functioning to the point that we rather speak today of "democracy of opinion," that is to say of a "media democracy, direct and permanent."[18]

---

[18] Jacques Julliard, *La Reine du monde: essai sur la démocratie d'opinion*, Paris: Flammarion, 2008, p. 107.

But did this not come about as a reaction to a representative democracy operating in an oligarchic mode between elections? The reproduction of the ruling castes, and above all the improvement, within these castes of collective power, of strategies based no longer simply on contempt or the illusion of superiority, but on a fear that grows just as inequality widens, which pushes them—consciously or not—to work shamelessly toward a culture of submission. Has all this not alienated them from their voters and their aspirations to have a share in the citizens' debate?

Oligarchy, today, means intermediate technobureaucracy, with its obligatory procession of experts, of more or less orchestrated media leaks, of the constitution of undue privileges for the few, and profound modifications of the relations between elected officials and voters. The people therefore have the often well-founded impression that their representatives no longer belong to them, and constitute a full-fledged class that does not facilitate democratic functioning. Hence the current feeling of rejection of a political class responsible for representing the people within the framework of an expected democratic operation.

Thus, even if it is highly likely that most of the people elected will fulfill their missions correctly and honestly, the idea that "the political class is corrupt" is constantly imposed, constituting for the authoritarian parties a cheap bargain—adding further cause for concern among ruling elites and professionals, pushing them to strengthen their independence from the people—and also fueling controversy over democracy itself. This issue becomes a real challenge that must be understood in order to resolve it and overcome it democratically, so as not to fall into the trap hatched by the forces riding on populism.

Another element seems important to consider: The radical change that appeared during the generalization of "the defense of human rights," which has gradually replaced the idea of a collective—albeit necessary for the articulation of relations between citizens—has at the same time legitimized a fierce contemporary individualism under the guise of inexpensive good feelings. For Marcel Gauchet,[19] human rights are still not a policy (*politique*), they do not succeed in ensuring a hold on the social, but remain a "politics" of collective powerlessness:

> The current problem is that they have become not only politics, but the whole of politics, both the "organizing norm of collective consciousness" and "the standard of political action." This is why human rights reveals a deep political malaise in democracy, a malaise whose source lies at the very heart of democratic ideals. In short, the unease of a democracy instituting itself against itself.[20]

Through his work, Marcel Gauchet helps us to better understand the roots of the clear conscience generalized by a frenzied self-esteem, built on the rubble of a democracy once imagined by the Encyclopédistes as a collective of citizens free and equal in law.

Such an observation leads us to think that, despite its democratic ambitions, politics has come to mean the service of a few, rather than Churchill's "least bad system" of government in the service of all. Returning to such paradigms in the current climate can only be contemplated by "the reinvestment of the political function by a new generation of citizens, eager to repair its deficiencies, and to defend against all odds the democratic values and the common good."[21]

---

[19] Marcel Gauchet, *La Démocratie contre elle-même*, Paris: Gallimard, 2002, p. 330.
[20] Martin Breaugh, "*Recension de la démocratie contre elle-même*", in *Politique et sociétés*, vol. 21, no. 3, 2002, pp. 173–180.
[21] Laurent Cohen-Tanugi, *Résistances: la démocratie à l'épreuve*, Paris: L'Observatoire, 2017, p. 117.

The recent questioning of such a pattern in several countries (among others: Russia, Turkey, Venezuela), made possible after seemingly legal takeovers by elected officials acceding to the status of quasi-monarchs, playing with the democratic rule of alternation, only make our reflections on this crucial subject even more sensitive.

CHAPTER TWO

Media, opinions, images

In these developments, the media have played and are playing an essential role. In certain cases, they hold a positive influence: that of a true fourth power raising the debate to a desirable level by providing elements of information likely to help citizens to form a personal point of view, and hence the voters to choose the candidate representing their aspirations. On the other hand, the sordid ultra-mediatization of the most mediocre aspects of special-interest calculations obscures the debate with advertising effects intended to "sell," for example, the candidate of a powerful lobby, often having considerable financial means, when it is not to slander any candidature likely to upset the patterns by which our elites are consolidated.

The opinions (*doxa*) resulting in part from what information is available to the people on which to base their judgment,[22] in turn, help to consolidate the legitimacy of the powerful ... or not! But if it is manipulated in a perverse way, the culture of opinion, in and of itself (with the sole end of its own inflation), can hamper the exercise of the institutions of representative democracy through political interventions, whether they be direct (demonstrations, petitions against a background of demagoguery) or indirect (lobbying or corruption strategy, planned disinformation). The point here is not to question the right to demonstrate and to strike, which are part of constitutional rights, but rather to draw attention to the media manipulation to which they may be subject, intended to "buy" an often malleable opinion. Pascal, considering democracy as "the science of consent to power,"[23] puts opinion in its proper place:

> The empire based on opinion and imagination reigns for some time, and this empire is gentle and willful. That of force still reigns. So, opinion is like the queen of the world, but strength is its tyrant.[24]

Under these conditions, the images that politicians present in the media become the ultimate weapon by which they are elected, by directing opinions, for better or for worse, whatever the relationship between these images and the words and deeds of these politicians may be. And once invested in this way, this inauthentic image contains all the characteristics of the "false self"

---

[22] This is the function of the newspaper, about which Gabriel Tarde speaks in his masterful sociological work, *Les lois de l'imitation* (1890).
[23] Jacques Julliard, *La Reine du monde*, op. cit., p. 49.
[24] Blaise Pascal, ed. Philippe Sellier, *Pensées, textes choisis*, Paris: Le Seuil, 1976, re-ed. 2009, p. 546.

described by Winnicott in his studies of normal and pathological personalities.

Of course, it is heartbreaking to note that the current democratic system awards a special bonus to these candidates, by ceding to them the power that their infantile omnipotence intends to hold in order to satisfy the inflation of their "egos," rather than any other mission at the service of their constituents, the voters of a declining democracy.

Little by little, coming to power and keeping it relies on the image that one diffuses; or even on knowing how to "sell" oneself (an expression that has become common among *coaches* of all kinds). One would expect, in a democracy, that elections would be won at the end of public debates on a project or program, orientations to it, and the means proposed to achieve it by one who is in line with the majority of voters, and not on the model of an auction of the most attractive images. But the new techniques of power accessible by unscrupulous political figures are constantly being improved by analyzing, through surveys, the feedback effects of advertisements which always flatter the greatest possible number of "spectator voters." They are also the result of the exploitation of "available brain time" for the new political neuroeconomics, starting from the realization of the possibility of influencing voters through the same channels as those of commercial advertising.

We can clearly see how non-conflicting manipulative seductions spread, while democratic forms of well-argued and conflictual debate—taking into account the reality of our contemporary *socius* and what needs to be changed in human terms to ensure its sustainability for the greater number—come to be aware of the opprobrium and censorship of the "controversial subject," unfit for the reign of a single, consensual, secure, and generalized opinion.

Without really foreseeing this radical change, our Western societies pass insensibly from representative democracy to media democracy, in which policies are more and more the playthings of constraints imposed by the extreme financialization of international capitalism at the service of the most powerful. An "overwhelming minority" of endlessly wealthy people objectively weighs in on the destinies of our planet. Politicians "elected" on their images and their "false self" programs will, by definition, be incapable of changing anything deeply troubling in this world, in particular with regard to two fundamental elements: the outrageous development of the distribution of wealth, and the ecological recklessness of the majority of rulers. This is without counting the political regimes that are more akin to what Mermet names "democratorship,"[25] or even more or less overt totalitarian regimes.

Obviously, democracy as we could have imagined it during the good times of its invention, the search for its improvement, and its desirable developments are no longer on the agenda: we are now in a Republic of the False Self.

---

[25] Gérard Mermet, *Démocrature: comment les médias transforment la démocratie*, Paris: Aubier, 1987, p. 7.

CHAPTER THREE

But what is a false self?

In the development of the child, one of the fundamental tasks is to achieve a relative balance between the internal urge-based world, governed by the principle of pleasure/displeasure, and the restrictions of the reality principle, which limit the child's all-powerful infantile state through "the interiorization of the philosophical category of the other."[26] To do this, the child gradually internalizes what he has received from his parents and from the social group in which he lives in constant interaction, like so many rules of the game or lines of conduct, in order to stem the impulsive force which would push him towards the assumption of a self-centered infantile omnipotence.

---

[26] Pierre Delion, *Le développement de l'enfant expliqué aux enfants d'aujourd'hui*, Toulouse: Érès, 2013.

Freud suggested that we keep these forces in equilibrium by representations existing in each human being. The instincts (*pulsions*) are represented by the "id," essentially unconscious; the parental heritage by the instance of the "superego;" and the body responsible for balancing the forces present by the "ego" or "me." From this perspective, the ego, or self,[27] is the seat of our consciousness, even if a part is overdetermined by the unconscious. This achievement is the result of a long evolution that lasts throughout childhood and adolescence and matures into adulthood.

In this evolutionary process, the image that represents me, built around the famous "mirror stage" discovered by Henri Wallon and taken up by Jacques Lacan, is essentially of an imaginary texture. It corresponds to my idea of myself, based on who I really am, my desires, my ideals, and my limits. As we can see, this situation requires compromise, ceaselessly in search of a balance between instinctual forces, between the hopes for an often unattainable ideal and the limits imposed by an inescapable reality.

When, for complex reasons related to psychopathology, the infant is born in an environment that does not present the qualities necessary for an "ordinary" development, then, rather than generating this balance and compromise with the forces in his presence, he will build, in order to adapt his relationship with (or survive) a reality from which he is not sufficiently protected by "good-enough" parental functions,[28] a defensive body which resembles the "me" or the "self," but is not authentic. Winnicott coined the concept of "false self" to qualify such a defensive creation of the infant and toddler.

---

[27] Psychopathologists note a difference between me and self, but this is not the object in question here.

[28] This allusion to the *"good-enough mother"* described by Winnicott, Joyce McDougall prefers to be translated as "adequate mother without more," so as not to "moralize" the qualities essential to development.

Imagine an infant who must survive in a parental environment that does not provide adequate responses to his physical and psycho-affective needs. The infant will build himself taking these deficiencies into account, as long as he has sufficient energy to do so, to change his environment: *When I need something (hunger, sleep, cleanliness, affection), I seem to be satisfied with the responses of my environment, and my "false self smile" replaces the crying which should express the needs of my true self.*

This emergence the false self can make people who are in charge of this child think that finally, despite the difficulties encountered in his "breeding," he is satisfied with what is brought to him. This is what the clinic teaches us under the term "hypermaturity" of deficient children, especially when they develop in an insecure environment.[29] Experience shows us that when these signs appear, the child ends up collapsing sooner or later, when the energy he had to fight against the effects of these deficiencies on him is exhausted: "The use of defenses, especially that of a successful false self, allows many children to appear promising, but in the end a collapse reveals that the true self is missing from the scene."[30]

Winnicott emphasizes the importance of inadequate parenting, since, from his perspective, "a life based on the cumulative effects of reactions to environmental encroachment, results in a life of false self, which is not life at all."[31]

These development mechanisms lead later to a double abnormality:

---

[29] The attachment theory invented by Bowlby distinguishes two types of environment, secure and insecure, depending on whether the responses are adapted or not for the baby.

[30] Donald W. Winnicott, trans. Jeannine Kalmanovitch, "*Distorsion du moi en fonction du vrai et du faux-self*" (1960), in *Processus de maturation chez l'enfant*, Paris: Payot, 1970, pp. 115–132.

[31] Donald W. Winnicott, trans. Jeannine Kalmanovitch, "*De la communication à la non-communication*" (1963), in *Processus de maturation chez l'enfant*, op. cit., pp. 151–168.

(1) the false self, organized to mask the true self, and
(2) an attempt on the part of the individual to solve his personal problem using the subtlety of his intellect. This results in a particular clinical picture because it is easily misleading. One can observe in such an individual a high level of academic success, and it is hard to believe the very real distress of one who feels most like a "charlatan" when he succeeds. That such individuals destroy themselves in one way or another, instead of fulfilling their promise, always shocks those who put great hopes in them.[32]

And the great English psychoanalyst deduces long-term consequences: "Morality or the lack of it is linked to living a true or false self."[33] It further specifies that "the absence of morality in babies consists in submitting to others, at the expense of a personal way of life."[34]

In doing so, the baby acts in accordance with the notion of voluntary servitude,[35] lending precocious origins to the development of certain children. All these developments proposed by Winnicott can be usefully compared to the work of Racamier on narcissistic perversion, shedding light on the working of this key concept in the problematic functioning of our contemporary societies.[36]

But in the development of the contemporary child, a new factor must also be taken into consideration, because it multiplies the effects previously described: These effects are exacerbated in

---

[32] Donald W. Winnicott, "*Distorsion du moi …* ", op. cit., p. 144.

[33] Jan Abram, trans. Cléopâtre Athanassiou, *Le langage de Winnicott*, Paris: Popesco, 2001, p. 330.

[34] Donald W. Winnicott, trans. Jeannine Kalmanovitch, "*Morale et éducation*" (1963), in *Processus de maturation…* , op. cit., p. 102.

[35] Cf. Étienne de La Boétie, *Discours de la servitude volontaire* (1548), re-ed. Paris: Payot, 2002.

[36] Cf. Paul-Claude Racamier, *Les perversions narcissiques*, Paris: Payot, 2012, which is a posthumous reprise of *Le génie des origines* (1992).

children who spend more than four hours a day in front of screens. By doing so, children profoundly change their relationship with the reality of the world that welcomes them. Recent work shows that the consequences observed as a function of exposure time in front of screens are manifested by sharply increasing symptoms: hyperactivity, attention disorders, obesity, violence.[37]

To satisfy his scopic impulse, the child is ready to spend hours looking at the screen, thus sacrificing the construction of his body image, in particular in its relationship with motor and then psychomotor expression, which indicate how to act in a world with three dimensions. The image itself opens onto a two-dimensional world and leads these children directly toward the virtual without sufficiently experiencing the possibilities of the body, which does not help them in the necessary compromise with the reality principle.

The image watched is, in fact, an object of considerable investment by the child in terms of time and energy, to the detriment of the dimension of the game which, for the moment, remains the best means to grow cognitively and psycho-affectively (for example, the market for video games supposed to make children smarter faster).

The child of our day also develops a false self, but with strands other than those used by deprived children described earlier. It is constructed upon and with images in a hypertrophic way, thus reinforcing a lack of balance between these images and the developing subject. What unites them is the growing gap between, on the one hand, the societal importance granted to self-image, and, on the other hand, the casualness displayed by our contemporaries *vis-à-vis* the subjective authenticity on which the self is built.

Here again, it is not a question of defending the idea of a society made up of perfect citizens deemed to be "authentic," disregarding

---

[37] Cf. especially Serge Tisseron, *Apprivoiser les écrans et grandir*, Toulouse: Érès, 2013.

the dark side of man (which could end in some illusory paradise, true expression of puritan fantasies at the origin of many totalitarian regimes), but to recall that the credit given to the notion of authenticity is equivalent to the degree of recognition of the difficulties inherent in the process of humanization in each one of us, which also undergirds the psychotherapeutic process.

CHAPTER FOUR

Societal changes in relation to the inflation of the image

As we can see, the false self is a defense which consists, from the start of a child's development, of showing himself in an appearance that does not correspond to the reality of who he is. If we can understand that for a child living in a deprived environment (qualitatively and/or quantitatively), it is impossible to do otherwise to survive physically and psychically. For a "child of screens," the interaction with the world has been significantly changed, and we can remark on the difference between this child and a person who has become an adult, often endowed with a beautiful intelligence, who continues to defend himself in the manner of what he experienced as a child when he has reached a position which no longer requires it. The representation of oneself by the false self has been, since the exponential development of a culture based essentially on images, encouraged by a profound societal movement to which great authors have drawn our attention. These references are by no means exhaustive, but let us allow the reflection to be anchored in the thinking of known and recognized people.

Guy Debord, in his work on *La Société du Spectacle*,[38] explains that the critical concept of "spectacle" is not a set of images, but a social relationship between people, mediated by images. We are therefore very much a part of imaginary existence, the ego/self/me which represents the person, and the intersubjective relations becoming, or even reducing themselves to, a game of images within the framework of a vast societal theater which stands out from a reality embodied in people. Debord therefore does not deal with the "spectacle" through the ages, but makes it an essential characteristic of contemporary society, which has become for him a vast spectacle. For him, the theory of the spectacle should be linked to the question of the analysis of the commodity, of reification, of the value and the fetishism of the commodity, as it was developed by Marx. Giorgio Agamben, in his afterword to the edition of Debord's works in Italy, showed how premonitory this author's vision was:

> Perhaps the most disturbing aspect of Debord's books is the relentlessness with which history seems to have applied itself to confirming his analyses. It is not only that twenty years after "The Society of the Spectacle," the "Comments on the Society of the Spectacle" (1988) has been able to record in all fields the accuracy of his diagnoses and forecasts, but in the meantime, the course of events has accelerated everywhere so uniformly in the same direction, that barely two years after the publication of the book, it seems

---

[38] Guy Debord, *La Société du Spectacle*, Paris: Buchet-Chastel, 1967.

that world politics today is no more than a parody of the scenario that it contained.[39]

A second author, Dany-Robert Dufour, in his book *Le Divin Marché*, shows

> the potentially devastating effects of the liberal principle, not only in the market economy, but also and above all in the other great human economies: political, symbolic, semiotic and psychic economies—without forgetting the one which encompasses them all, the economy of the living.

In *La Cité perverse: libéralisme et pornographie*, he strives to show that the economic and financial crisis that appeared in October 2008 exposed the perverse mechanisms that now govern the functioning of the City:

> Pornography, egotism, contestation of any law, acceptance of social Darwinism, instrumentalization of the other: our world has become about Sade. It now celebrates the alliance of Adam Smith and the Marquis of Sade.[40]

Dufour tries to show that, for the old moral order which commanded everyone to repress their impulses and desires, a new order has been substituted that encourages them to exhibit them, whatever the consequences. This exhibition, in fact, relies on the society of the spectacle as it is explained by Debord. And this exhibition can only be produced by using self-image, which has therefore become equivalent to a false self-image in many instances.

---

[39] Giorgio Agamben, Postface in the Italian edition of *La Société du Spectacle*, Rome: 1990.
[40] Id., *La Cité perverse: libéralisme et pornographie*, Paris: Denoël, 2009.

His last work achieves an admirable synthesis of all these phenomena and calls for finding a "middle and final path to rebuild the role of the State and to rebuild the social bond" from a "universalist principle."[41]

Taking a step aside, a third author interests us in this research concerning the functions of images in the development of humans: Yal Ayerdhal, science fiction writer. His novel, *La Bohême et l'Ivraie* tells us about a world in which the projection of images has become the *ne plus ultra* of culture.[42] The hero of the cycle is a Kinéïre, an artist able to project his emotions, images, and sounds into the minds of people to the point where they confuse them with their true memories. Rejected from Kinéïrat school for non-conformism, he learns to master his powers and take them to an unparalleled degree, to the point that he worries even the powerful Ethics Committee and its leader. In this anticipatory novel, the importance of "imposed" images in societal organization is brought to a climax, which gives us food for thought about the effects of such a hold on human societies and their future.

---

[41] Id., *Du déclin au réveil de l'intérêt général*, Bruxelles: Yapaka.be, coll. "*Temps d'arrêt*", 2018.
[42] Yal Ayerdhal, *La Bohême et l'Ivraie*, Paris: *Fleuve noir*, coll. "*Anticipation*", 1990.

CHAPTER FIVE

Discomfort in the helping relationship

As we have seen, media democracy favors spectacle to the detriment of reality, and finds legitimacy in the first to better escape the second. We also found that the actors in these spectacles were too often false-self personalities. We have understood, with the help of several thinkers, that the spectators of these inauthentic encounters were themselves more concerned with their own narcissism than with a hypothetic common good, even a "common" good in the sense given to it by Dardot and Laval.[43] Alain Deneault is even more explicit: "Freedom of expression comes at a price and it is the price paid by the rights-holders of unlimited property to capture it through the media."[44]

---

[43] Pierre Dardot, & Christian Laval, *Commun: essai sur la révolution au XXIe siècle*, Paris: La Découverte, 2014.
[44] Alain Deneault, *Faire l'économie de la haine*, Montréal: Écosociété, coll. "*Polémos*", 2018, p. 11.

These findings, painful as they are, are visible in many areas of our contemporary societies. But if there is one area in which the damage caused is devastating, it is that of the helping relationship.

Of course, the prison often makes the headlines for the outrageous conditions in which incarcerated people are mistreated. It is not a question here of throwing stones at the prison staff who have so few means to remain human amid the inhuman treatment observed and denounced by successive "defenders of freedoms;" they cannot be held accountable without considering criminal policy as a whole. More recently, it is the living conditions of dependent elderly people that have led the media to take an interest in the overwhelming testimony of staff who care for them despite cruel constraints.

In recent times, psychiatric caregivers have finally been able to be heard—time will tell if they have been listened to—about the unbearable conditions in which the mentally ill are today badly cared for, badly treated, and ill-considered by our health system.[45] We read almost daily, in *Le Monde* in particular, testimonies on the distress of staff: "Crushed by budgetary restrictions, caregivers say they are at the end of their rope and denounce a 'loss of meaning' in their work."[46]

Here again, there is no question of giving over to popular indignation the caregivers who are unable to do anything about the situation. Rather, we must try to understand the root of this inconsistency of the state, long denounced by the representatives of a disaster-stricken profession—the psychiatrists and their teams—their scientific groups, and their united federations.

---

[45] A hunger strike was declared by some caregivers at the Rouvray hospital near Rouen (May–June 2018) to denounce these scandalous conditions of care for the mentally ill. We can measure the ethical commitment of caregivers by such actions.

[46] François Béguin, "*Psychiatrie, le cri d'alarme des soignants*", in *Le Monde*, January 27, 2018, pp. 12–13.

An even more recent article may provide interesting avenues for thought in order to understand what is in question in hospital settings. Catherine Vincent describes "… isolated caregivers, placed in competition, unable to do their job well: Applied indiscriminately since the early 2000s, management methods from the private sector are a disaster for health and social institutions."[47]

Further on, she quotes Danièle Linhart: "It is unbearable for a doctor to be told by a manager how long an appointment with a schizophrenic should last."

And she adds:

> This management method, by bringing the hospital into a purely accounting logic, generates paradoxical situations and in particular leads to a decline in the autonomy and power of professionals. In a medical environment characterized by a strong autonomy of the actors, an environment having professional values and a strong code of ethics, this is not acceptable.

These distressing facts are observed in all French hospitals today, and their considerable effects on the quality of care are now known. But in a field such as psychiatry, where the quality of the relationship between caregivers and patients is so decisive for the conditions of care, the above-described effects have even more distressing consequences, as the position of caregivers rests on a welcoming function (*fonction d'accueil*) legitimized by the state.

When Bonnafé declared in his time that "The behavior of a society with its lunatics is one of the best testimonies of its degree of civilization,"[48] he insisted on the fact that those who take care of

---

[47] Catherine Vincent, "*Le soin saccagé. L'hôpital malade du management*", in *Le Monde des idées*, February 17, 2018, pp. 1–3.
[48] Lucien Bonnafé, "*L'idiot révélateur*", in *Esprit* no. 11, November 1965, p. 628.

the mentally ill must be supported absolutely by the state, precisely because it is the tendency of Western societies to reject them, even under the guise of support and empathy.

Social alienation, explored by Marx, then taken up by Tosquelles, Bonnafé, Oury, and others to make it one of the key concepts of sector psychiatry,[49] must be taken into consideration in order to avoid its pitfalls.[50]

It is only when this social alienation is taken into account that psychopathological alienation can find answers *a posteriori*, in psychotherapeutic approaches. Otherwise, we fall into the lures of antipsychiatry, singularly lacking in nuance, which attributed to asylum and reactionary psychiatrists full responsibility for ordinary madness.

However, hospital "management," the casualness of the detractors of sector psychiatry, the inequity of budgets devoted to medicine and psychiatry, the increasingly biologizing training of psychiatrists, and the disregard of the phenomena of transfers specific to the mentally ill are all reasons which lead caregivers today to feel abandoned, disqualified, and mistreated by their superiors.

How can we still claim to treat the psychic suffering of disturbed persons under these conditions? In spite of ourselves, we will not be able to continue to endorse, nor to exercise, this institutional violence and objective mistreatment.[51]

This line of questioning, which is certainly radical, concerns itself with nothing more or less than reconnecting with the subjectivity of human beings, starting with those who present proven psychopathological suffering.

---

[49] Cf. Jean Oury, *L'Aliénation, Séminaire of Sainte-Anne 1990–1991*, Paris: Galilée, 1992.
[50] Cf. Élie Pouillaude, *L'Aliénation: psychose et psychothérapie institutionnelle*, Paris: Hermann, 2014.
[51] Cf. Thierry Najimann, *Lieu d'asile: manifeste pour une autre psychiatrie*, Paris: Odile Jacob, 2015.

CHAPTER SIX

Is there still a subject in man?

In 1986, François Tosquelles argued that "Without the recognition of the human value of madness, it is man himself who disappears."[52] Coming to his rescue, Henri Maldiney declared in 1999, with the power that characterizes him, that "Man is increasingly absent from psychiatry; but few notice it, because man is more and more absent from man."[53]

We cannot say with certainty what is happening to us and against what we must fight collectively, with all our ethical, intellectual, and emotional forces. It is not a question of a Romantic or aesthetic attitude—which might suggest a nostalgic or even depressive position—but a movement that brings together all

---

[52] François Tosquelles, "*Avant-propos à l'édition de 1986*", in *Le vécu de la fin du monde dans la folie*, re-ed. Grenoble: Jérôme Millon, 2012.
[53] Henri Maldiney, "*L'homme dans la psychiatrie*", in *Revue de Psychothérapie psychanalytique de groupe*, n° 36, 2001/1, pp. 31–46.

the scattered elements that only the history of psychiatry sheds light on: the reality of its deleterious errors and of the hopes of its unfinished revolutions.

It must be said loud and clear: a certain idea of psychiatry prevailed for several decades, which made it possible to achieve profound changes in its practice with people affected by this unique pathology.

And all of this could simply disappear? And, what is more, for the wrong reasons? What holds for person-to-person psychiatry also holds true for democracy: we only realize its immense importance when it becomes at risk of disappearing, both its precarious nature and the fragility of the checks and balances imbricated in the history of our countries and our daily lives, although threatened at every moment of being driven out by disintegrative forces.

It is not easy to admit that human progress can never be taken for granted once and for all. And the correspondence between Freud and Einstein reminds us that the processes of idealization, considering the destructiveness of man as amendable, are our worst enemies on the path of civilization for human beings in themselves (*l'hommelui-même*), which, through cultural processes, is alone capable of transforming violence.[54]

It is only when one is well aware of the (material and subjective) limits of human civilization that an evaluation of the forces present is possible in reality. Otherwise, the traps of imaginary inflation close in on utopias before they can come into being. This is in part what happens to our "transferential psychiatry," for having failed to explain itself sufficiently or by dint of neglecting the expectations of "secure psychiatry." Our contemporary *socius*, then, steeped in discomfort created by short-sighted demagogues,

---

[54] Sigmund Freud, *Pourquoi la guerre? Correspondance avec Albert Einstein*, in *Œuvres complètes*, vol. XIX (1931–1936), trans. Janine Altounian, André Bourguignon, Pierre Cotet, & Alain Rauzy, Paris: PUF, 2004, pp. 309–314.

morons of pseudo-science excited by increasingly over-simplified and complacent media, will prefer as much to the humanization of its modes of exercise.

From a certain point of view, especially through "freeze-dried assessment processes,"[55] a war against humanity in relational practices has been declared; and psychiatry, with pedagogy, education, justice, social work, and other great comparable causes, is at the forefront of this fight.

For a psychiatry without a subject is a deadly psychiatry.

---

[55] Cf. Roland Gori, Barbara Cassin, & Christian Laval, *"L'Appel des appels, pour une insurrection des consciences"*, Paris: Fayard, 2009.

CHAPTER SEVEN

The psychiatric revolution

Before exploring the avatars of today's psychiatry in greater depth, which risks closing in on its known and unknown demons, it seems useful to me to browse the history of its evolutions and revolutions to better perceive the origin of the forces that preside over the restoration of the subject in man. The psychiatric revolution begins with Pinel and Pussin, on the shoulders of the Encyclopédistes, and in the wake of the French Revolution. The madman is a citizen, and as such, the doctor can help him; he is thus freed from the prisons and dead-end pits in which he previously languished by royal decree; the now "mentally ill" person has the right to be treated in an attempt at humanizing understanding, by a "moral treatment" which is based on a revolutionary philosophical position.

But this pioneering position—understood differently by Foucault,[56] by Gauchet and Swain,[57] and, more recently, by Laure Murat[58]—largely due to the charisma of its two first founders, will gradually reveal itself in the reforms by Esquirol on spaces dedicated to the mentally ill, to the detriment of the art of inhabiting them with humanity. The law of 1838 begins with this foundation: "An asylum for the insane is created in each *departement*,"[59] a legislative translation of Esquirol's operational thinking, for whom this new space constitutes "an instrument of healing: In the hands of a skilled physician, it is the most powerful therapeutic agent against mental illness."[60]

Once the brief honeymoon following this achievement had passed, obliterating the relational and truly intersubjective character that the utopia of moral treatment suggested—and erasing its liberating potential in the now famous "asylum walls"—experience has shown that without the inspiration which guided the first philosopher-psychists, this location of madness in medicalized places was simply doomed to fail owing to the unconscious transference.

In the aftermath, we understood that without the Freudian invention—rehabilitating the world of neuroses and allowing the discovery of the power of transference to better approach the infantile in the actuality of its relation to the world—the trap of insanity could not be avoided without recourse to unconscious overdetermination.

This first stage of these developments only partially answered the questions posed by the fates of asylums, in so far as the

---

[56] Cf. Michel Foucault, *Histoire de la folie à l'âge classique* (1961), Paris: Gallimard, 1972.

[57] Cf. Marcel Gauchet, & Gladys Swain, *La Pratique de l'esprit humain. L'institution asilaire et la révolution démocratique,* Paris: Gallimard, 1980.

[58] Cf. Laure Murat, *L'Homme qui se prenait pour Napoléon: pour une histoire politique de la folie,* Paris: Gallimard, 2011.

[59] "*Loi du 30 juin 1838 sur les d'aliénés*", in *Bulletin des Lois* no. 7443.

[60] Jean-Étienne Esquirol, *Des maladies mentales considérées sous le rapport médical, hygiénique et médico-légal,* volume II, Paris: J.-B. Baillières, 1838, p. 398.

transference of neurotic persons had little to do with those of psychotic people, stuck in an institution for the insane. It was not until a few decades more and the onset of World War II that Freudian metapsychology was revisited by the fathers of institutional psychotherapy, more precisely by François Tosquelles and then by Jean Oury.

Transposing Freudian discoveries by rethinking them in the light of the pathologies confronted in a psychiatric environment, we can observe precisely how a closed-off space can never succeed in transforming (in Bion's sense) the elements of double alienation—psychopathological and social—which, previously existing in the *socius*, will have led the patient to the asylum. This is how, in the asylums themselves, when this phenomenon is not taken into account, we observe the reproduction of the same alienation mechanisms: segregation, compartmentalization, isolation, pathoplasty, and sedimentation.

For example, in an enclosed space, the less pathological people will tend to consider the most pathological as bad company and thus reject them in turn: a segregation between the patients is then organized by the asylum, that is, by those who work there as caregivers as well as by the patients themselves. The resulting compartmentalization reinforces the isolation of the sickest. Significant symptoms of this institutional abandonment (bedwetting, bodily-psychic regression, hospitalism, motor and psycho-emotional withdrawal, generalized violence, etc.) then emerge and come to confirm the idea that these individuals are really even sicker than expected. And the only solution seen by professionals with little training in iatrogenic pathologies is retreat to "the pavilions at the back of the hospital" and asylum sedimentation,[61] real psychic death while awaiting physical death.

---

[61] Cf. Louis Le Guillant, Lucien Bonnafé, & Hubert Mignot, "*Problèmes posés par la chronicité sur le plan des institutions psychiatriques*", in Pierre Warot (dir.), *Congrès de psychiatrie et de neurologie de langue française, LXIIe session, Comptes rendus*, vol II, Paris: Masson, 1964, pp. 1335–1711.

If, for Freud, the subject of neurosis is not where one expects it ("*Wo Es war, soll Ich werden*"—"Where id was, there the ego shall be"), it is because it is overdetermined by the unconscious, and, to a lesser extent, by the superego, both of which maintain instinctual power relations with the ego that produce the symptoms of average occidental neurosis. In some cases, the forces in question overwhelm the capacities of the system and trigger a pathological neurosis, but the two innovative Freudian ideas are that even in such occurrences: (1) there is no definitive difference between the normal and the pathological, and (2) symptoms have a meaning for the subject stuck in his normal or pathological neurosis: it is up to the psychoanalyst, who has become a sleuth of the origins of psychological suffering, to find its meaning, not in the place of the patient, but with him, co-actor of his therapy. To achieve this, Freud advises reliance on the relationship between patient and psychoanalyst shaped by the subjective experience of the patient's childhood and to actualize in the "here and now" his first interactions with his parents during his infantile period; in other words, on the transference.

The Freudian project is to restore the subject in man, even at the cost of his neurotic madness. And it is unbearable to hear that institutional psychotherapy would not have the objective of restoring the subject in the psychotic man and in the autistic child,[62] while granting him all the time necessary in the establishment. But the typical treatment has its limits, in particular when it comes to treating psychotic people and submitting to their singular forms of transference, in particular, dissociated transference (a specific form of transference in schizophrenia described by Oury), but also the psychotic/projective transference and the autistic/adhesive

---

[62] The H.A.S. recommendations of June 2012 on the management of autistic children formally contraindicate the use of psychoanalysis and institutional psychotherapy.

transference and their obligatory corollaries, the transferential constellations of each patient, with institutional establishments responding to each patient's specific "being-in-the-world."

Institutional psychotherapy was born in part from the answer to the question posed by a visionary Freud at the conclusion of the Fifth International Psychoanalytic Congress in Budapest taking place on the heels of the First World War, by suggesting, without formulating it so clearly, that the institution be the missing link in the establishment of the transferential relationship between the psychotic patient and the caregivers who receive him, and by considering the deployment of this institution to be such that the human being is cultivated there in the prevailing manner. I cannot resist here the need to quote this excerpt from Freud:

> In conclusion, I want to consider a situation which is in the realm of the future and which many of you will consider to be fanciful, but which in my opinion is worth preparing our minds for. You know that the field of our therapeutic action is not very wide [...]
>
> One can foresee that, one day, social consciousness will awaken and remind the community that the poor have the same rights to psychological help as to the medical aid which is already provided to them by life-saving surgery. Society will also recognize that public health is no less threatened by neuroses than by tuberculosis [...]
>
> At that time, establishments and clinics will be built, headed by qualified psychoanalyst doctors and where, with the help of analysis, we will strive to return resistance and activity to men who otherwise would indulge in drinking, women who would succumb under the weight of frustrations, children who have no choice but between depravity and neurosis [...].

We will then be forced to adapt our technique to these new conditions.[63]

It is an understatement to say that institutional psychotherapy is a response to this important Freudian quasi-prophecy made in 1918.

---

[63] Sigmund Freud, "*Conclusions du cinquième congrès international psychanalytique de Budapest de septembre 1918*", in *La Technique psychanalytique*, trans. Anne Bermann, Paris, 1953.

CHAPTER EIGHT

Sector psychiatry and institutional psychotherapy

The creation of a genuine public psychiatry was then based, in France, on sector psychiatry and institutional psychotherapy designed and carried out in the crucible of Saint-Alban during and after the Second World War. It is the direct logical continuation of the first revolutionary acts of Pinel and Pussin, then of Freud: The subject in psychological suffering can now benefit from coherent and continuous care, offered as closely as possible to his place of existence and that of his relatives, and without implying hospitalization as a one-off remedy, but only a medical indication.

It is from the criticism of the living conditions of the sick, and in particular the death of 45,000 of them,[64] that the urgent

---

[64] Cf. Isabelle von Bueltzingsloewen, *L'Hécatombe des fous: la famine dans les hôpitaux psychiatriques français sous l'Occupation*, Paris: Aubier, 2007, re-ed. Flammarion, coll. "Champs", 2009.

need to restore respect for the subject in the sick man arises. The general awareness of this anthropological catastrophe facilitated the alliance with the political, and thus helped to shape the texts which would henceforth govern the system of public psychiatry.[65]

Meeting places with patients, either in or out of hospital, are then rearranged in the mode, proposed by Jean Ayme,[66] of a Möbius strip, which facilitates the continuity of care, a condition for the possibility of the transferential relationship. It is a matter of responding to the individual suffering of the subject with a psychotherapeutic approach in the broad sense, treating his psychopathological alienation, but without neglecting the elements of alienation which come from his position in the *socius* (family, work, culture). The subject in man—patient or therapist—is at the heart of this double alienation, which we then choose not to ignore in the political organization of care.

This requires recourse to the concept of "complementary reports" (taken up by Tosquelles at Dupréel[67]) which makes it possible to specify all the interactions and articulations necessary between the care provided by caregivers and the resource persons in the estate on which the patient continues to rely.

This specific work with patient-relays in the estate requires the commitment of the sector's own team to all those who can contribute to its support (family, friends, colleagues, teachers, etc.), but also to elected politicians, in order to modify citizens' impressions of mental illness.

---

[65] On the beginnings of the institutional psychotherapy movement, see in particular Jean Oury, *La Psychothérapie institutionnelle de Saint-Alban à La Borde*, Paris: Éditions d'une, 2016.

[66] Jean Ayme was a key player in the establishment of the sector through his role as president of the Syndicate of Hospital Psychiatrists. Cf. Jean Ayme, *Chroniques de la psychiatrie publique*, Toulouse: Érès, coll. "*Des travaux et des jours*", 1995.

[67] Cf. François Tosquelles, *Pédagogie et psychothérapie institutionnelle* (1966), re-ed. *Éducation et psychothérapie institutionnelle*, Nîmes: Champ Social, 2006.

For this, three "instances" are useful:

(1) The "institution," defined as a set of people united by a common mission—in this case, treating patients—developing the optimal conditions of possibility in a given context to fulfill its entrusted mission,[68] serves as a malleable intermediate object in the complex construction of a transferential constellation.[69] It is both flexible and plastic to be able to adapt sufficiently to each psychopathological situation, but its solidity makes it a *phoric* support on which the patient can count.[70]
(2) Then, the professional healthcare team, the group by which the transferential constellations are "recruited," is the place of change to achieve the objectives pursued. This change can take place through relevant initial training, continuing training "in perpetuity," institutional reflection to better adapt to the particularities of each patient subject (and in particular to each form of transference), and a self-organization of the system to facilitate the initiatives taken by each member of the team. When these factors are sufficiently elaborated and developed, the team can become a "collective."[71]

---

[68] Tosquelles makes a distinction between "establishment" and "institution." The first is what is created by the state to fulfill a mission, such as building a hospital to treat patients. But depending on the people who are recruited in this establishment, the missions will be fulfilled differently: for him, the institution is all these people who organize the work necessary to meet the objectives set, and can demonstrate, to do so, contextualized initiatives.

[69] The transferential constellation is the set of people in contact with a patient. It is the form closest to each patient, their "tailor-made institutional costume."

[70] Cf. Pierre Delion, *Fonction phorique*, holding *et institutions*, Toulouse: Érès, 2018. The phoric function consists in "carrying" the child all the time that he cannot carry himself. By extension, it is the appropriate instruction to caregivers with the patient who needs to be "supported" (surrounded, supported, taken care of) because of his mental illness.

[71] Cf. Jean Oury, *Le Collectif*, op. cit.

(3) Finally, working meetings are the real operators of these considerable changes. On the condition of watching over what facilitates speech in a system usually structured in a hierarchical statutory mode, working meetings can become a place for sharing information, decision-making, and emotional exchanges.

These innovative perspectives aimed to radically change the functioning of psychiatry, and called into question the privileges of those who had discretionary power over the healthcare teams and over the patients themselves. This generated resistance, leading to the dilution of sector psychotherapy/institutional psychotherapy (since everyone thought they were doing it) in favor of a kind of soft psychiatry toward which everyone turned, from their own more or less fetishized psychic territories, the "marquisats" decried by Lucien Bonnafé,[72] without sufficient consideration for the anthro-psychiatric (*anthropopsychitriques*) motives of the original sectoral doctrine.[73]

Indeed, such a psychiatry can only happen if, alongside the official system governing the functioning of hospitals, the conditions necessary for the specific functioning of "transference logic" are put in place. A subjective hierarchy based on the human skills of each member of the group is necessary to offer the patient a range of transferential possibilities such as to permit their deployment in the care situation;[74] otherwise, caregivers are torn between the roles assigned to their status and the functions that each of the patients makes them play in the transference.

---

[72] Cf. Éric Favereau, & Philippe Artières, "*Saint-Alban, une aventure de fous*", in *Libération*, August 2, 2016.

[73] Cf. Jean-Louis Feys, *L'Anthropopsychiatrie de Jacques Schotte*, Paris: Hermann, 2009.

[74] Cf. Pierre Delion, "*Thérapeutiques institutionnelles*", in *Encyclopédie médico-chirurgicale*, 37-930-G-10, 2001.

Not wanting to take into account this unique situation, intrinsic to the professions of "psychists," we expose caregivers to the risk of burnout or rejection of patients. The (demanding) training in psychopathology, personal psychoanalytic courses, and the learning of group techniques, to name but a few, are subject to hazards which, for some, take the form of what can be called a professional false self, sometimes to the point of caricature. The famous "self-authorization," proposed by Lacan in a precise context is still too often taken literally and gives rise to mediocrity in practice, including the postures of "psychoanalysts in false self," all of which gives ammunition to the detractors of the sector and of psychoanalysis.

But more generally, as Roland Gori perfectly demonstrates in *La Fabrique des imposteurs*,[75] it is social relations that are being impoverished: progressively nibbled away by a culture of the faked image, and based mainly on the paradigm of the magic mirror: "Mirror, mirror on the wall, am I still the fairest of them all?" For Gori:

> Nowadays the impostor in our societies is like a fish in water: making form prevail over substance, valuing means rather than ends, trusting appearance and reputation over work and probity, preferring audience rating to merit, opting for advantageous pragmatism rather than the courage of truth, choosing the opportunism of opinion rather than holding firm on values, practicing the art of illusion rather than emancipating the self through critical thinking, surrendering to false security procedures rather than risking love and creation. This is the environment where sham thrives!

In recent years, we have noted with concern, and now with dread, that the images our contemporaries claim to give of themselves have less and less connection with what they "really" are.

---

[75] Roland Gori, *La Fabrique des imposteurs*, Paris: Les liens qui libèrent, 2013.

If this observation is not entirely new, what is more is the fact that we are duped by this virtual level of reality and that the attribution of powers to our representatives by the mechanisms of democracy is itself invaded by the prevalence of the image. It is therefore not surprising, as we have seen previously, that politicians are caught up in this movement, and that, prisoners of their only image, their false self, they do not find the means to improve the daily life of their fellow citizens, since the elected person does not really correspond to who they authentically are.

Indeed, the represented elect representatives based on the strength of the latter's image and begin to realize that too often this image does not correspond to the reality of the person. Recent examples of a few unscrupulous politicians show over and over again that this gap—between the reality and the image—is problematic, because the people in question are absent from themselves when they agree to fulfill missions in which the gap will obviously appear and force them to resign.

But what is true for politicians can be extended to many levels of our society, and in particular to the professions of human relations, in which this "new attitude" leads to disastrous results with our sick contemporaries who have a real need to count on someone in order to be able to come out of their abandonment. Otherwise, it obviously reinforces their impression of being abandoned, they who have already experienced the weakening of an environment operating in an "insecure" mode in their childhoods.

The oppositions that sector psychiatry had managed to overcome (and which will earn it a programmed decline) have become the daily routine of psychiatric caregivers. Relations between psychiatrists and administrators are strained in a conflict over power as useless as it is deleterious. Permanent emergencies face chronically ill patients who are not sufficiently supported in their psychotic existence, too often installing the famous "revolving door syndrome."[76] Notions of autonomy and dependence are no longer included in a diachronic continuity of care, but are photographed at a single instant or time ("t"), to deduce operative services. The disease tends to disappear in the face of the all-powerful "handicap," a provider of allowances which are certainly necessary but enclosing each "disabled" person in a less dynamic status.

All of this is linked to a profound change in the apprehension of the symptoms presented by patients, now tending toward a purely behavioral reading in defiance of the underlying psychopathological structure.

This "involution" takes shape in the modes of international classifications governed by a statistical logic to the detriment of individual logic, the main consequence of which is the protocolized prescription of psychotropic drugs and cognitive behavioral techniques that are supposedly validated on the scientific level.

Conversely, psychoanalysis and its extensions,[77] not scientifically validated, are pushed to the margins of history with irresponsible casualness. However, numerous experiences of knowledgeable departments and teams practicing institutional psychotherapy clearly show all the benefits to be expected from such practices: in La Borde, in Reims (with Patrick Chemla, his team, and the patients mobilized around them), in Landerneau, Angers, Abbeville, Caen, Marseille, Perpignan, and many other places.

Another effect of this behavioralization of psychiatry is the creation of resource centers dedicated to the symptoms in question,[78]

---

[76] Bernard Castro et al., "The revolving door syndrome in psychiatry," *in Annales medico-psycholgiques,* vol. 165, no. 4, May 2007, pp. 276–281.

[77] Cf. René Kaës, *L'Extension de la psychanalyse: pour une métapsychologie du troisième type*, Paris: Dunod, 2015.

[78] Attention deficit disorder with or without hyperactivity, autism spectrum disorder, and dys-lexia, -praxia, -calculia, -phasia as listed in the *Diagnostic and Statistical Manual of Disorders.*

ignoring a genuinely medical and anthropological approach. The use of such specializations would be justified if requested by a primary care practitioner needing additional advice. But going through these "expert centers" most often becomes an inescapable demand. And in the same movement, expertise becomes ... truth.

All these divisions of psychiatric praxis ultimately lead to divisions that are institutionalized in concrete practices: as a specialist in such and such a symptom, I receive only the carriers of this symptom and am no longer required to provide a general welcome for all those who come to my consultation. They atomize psychiatry into a symptomatic sectorization worthy of a mail-order catalog, or even a Prévert-style inventory, unrelated to historical sectorization.

In addition, the de-medicalization of the functions necessary for the coherent functioning of psychiatric services continues and results in the constitution of services directed, in fact, by administrators often little inclined to listen to the specificities of psychiatry, in which professionals who are often poorly trained in this discipline, and organized in a very segregative mode, tend to freeze the subject in his presenting symptoms rather than recognizing as fluid his suffering toward polyphonic responses, based on a transferential coherence.

CHAPTER NINE

Medicine with a human face

Medicine with a human face has suffered from progressive specializations which have ultimately led to hyperspecialized medicine, known as organ medicine, sometimes without sufficient consideration for the subject carrying the disease.

But from the 1930s onwards, Michael Balint's entire effort consisted in building, with interested general practitioners, a return to the person.[79] When doctors can be helped in their ordinary work by returning to this notion of the person, which is essential for their ethics, most of the time they are satisfied with the quality that this experience gives to their practice. Moreover, we are currently witnessing in the United States the return of a medicine

---

[79] Cf. Michael Balint, trans. Jean-Paul Valabrega, *Le Médecin, son malade et la maladie*, Paris: PUF, 1960.

appropriately known as "narrative medicine,"[80] in which the person regains his status as a person responsible for his own history, and no longer as a victim of his fate as a patient. It is not impossible that the need for the return of personal medicine will ultimately be felt more acutely in a country where evidence-based medicine has imposed itself—and which has observed, alongside some (limited) progress in so-called "hard" medical specialties, the risks of lethal drought in others, especially in psychiatry!

But I would like to give two examples from my practice, as an indication, to show that this personal medicine doesn't cost anything other than making the decision:

(1) Obstetricians who, thanks to the consultation of the first trimester of pregnancy, can devote an hour to its psychological aspects, are affected by this typically human part which concerns the arrival of a child, with its core of hopes, but also of anguish. When the expectant mother can talk to her doctor about these elements, she "recovers" the human part of her medical adventure and feels more strongly equipped for what will happen to her. *A fortiori*, if depression or any other psychopathological phenomenon occurs during or after pregnancy, the doctor has elements of understanding which help him to help the mother in most cases. And when he needs more specialized advice from the psychiatrist, his address to his colleague is much more articulate. Groups of midwives and obstetricians, led by child psychiatrists, have been set up within the framework of perinatal networks, in which each practitioner can discuss a patient's story. These experiences show over and over again that these new practices respond to human needs which it is no longer acceptable to leave by the wayside on the pretext that they could mar the medical scientific process.

---

[80] François Goupy, & Claire Le Jeune (dir.), *La Médecine narrative: une révolution pédagogique?* Paris: Med-line Editions, 2016.

(2) Another example is that of research conducted with liberal pediatricians on the links between postnatal depression and functional signs in babies (insomnia, anorexia, early relationship disorders). The use of the Cox EPDS[81] scale in the pediatrician waiting room is used to assess the risk of depression in the mother. The pediatrician examines the baby and detects, or does not detect, the functional signs mentioned. If so, he looks at the mother's EPDS score and then looks at the mother's mental health. In 90% of cases, his interest in the health of the mother improves her depressive state and causes a regression of the functional signs of the baby. In 10%, the pediatrician sends the mother and her baby to her child psychiatrist colleague for a therapeutic consultation. It is really the pediatrician's emphasis on the importance of the mother which "re-narcissizes" her and enables her to come out of her postnatal depression, the symptoms of which the baby presented as partial effects.[82]

In these two experiments, the doctor's focus on the human aspects of situations has direct effects on the medical symptoms presented during the consultation. The subject is left out when the doctor contents himself with selecting his symptoms and treating them independently of any subjective position. Certainly, there are areas of medicine, in surgery for example, where an affective-emotional distancing process is required for technical reasons, but the return to the person, once the operation has been completed, must always be carried out for a human accompaniment.

---

[81] *Échelle de dépression postnatale d'Édimbourg (Edinburgh Postnatal Depression Scale).*
[82] Cf. Jean-François Lienhardt, & Francis Toursel, "*Existe-t-il une relation entre le risque de dépression post-natale et l'état de santé du bébé? Résultats d'une étude de la naissance à deux ans. Intérêt de la prévention de la dépression post-natale*", in *Archives de pédiatrie*, vol. 17, no. 6, append. 1, juin 2010, p. 22.

CHAPTER TEN

Human psychiatry

If, for medicine, this approach seems to go without saying (although many patients complain that it is still too rare), one would expect that in the field of psychiatry it would be part of a commonly accepted practice, rooted in its epistemic foundations. We recalled the history of psychiatry from the French Revolution. And we discovered to what extent the civilizing forces at work were often the result of other unbinding forces, seeking to atomize, compartmentalize, and serialize in order to operate in the "medicine of the soul" with new Linneo-Sydenhamian attempts, denounced in his time by Jacques Schotte as so many caricatures of applied science without the necessary adjustments to psychiatry.[83]

---

[83] Jean-Louis Feys, "*Quel système pour quelle classification psychiatrique? De Linné à Schotte, en passant par le DSM et Szondi*", in *Évolution psychiatrique*, vol. 79, no. 1, 2014, pp. 109–121.

However, these days, what do we see taking place, always under the cover of science, and more precisely evidence-based-medicine methods?[84] After having integrated, in an overly superficial way, the advances made possible by psychoanalytic psychopathology in medicine during the second half of the twentieth century, and having too often made it a fad that was talked about in authorized salons and in the same media which, today, despise it, to the detriment of real advances in the practice of care, psychoanalysis is experiencing a vengeful swing of the pendulum. We may see, as often in the fashions, certain so-called psychoanalysts, often self-authorized, leave this once honorable high ground to fall back on less complex methods, apparently more scientific, often cognitive-behavioral, thus proving their lack of interiorization of the previous methods!

These methods can prove to be useful, provided that they are given back the place they should never have left: that of education and re-education, which cannot be summed up by operant conditioning, which is a monoclonal caricature of it.

Today, there is a devastating confusion in the field of psychotherapy, that of an opposition between psychotherapy and cognitive behavioral therapies. The former are inspired by Pinel's moral treatment and deepen with Freud and psychoanalysis, including psychodrama, and various and varied psychotherapies. Institutional psychotherapy is, in this view, the general framework within which the various forms of psychotherapy can be practiced. In this regard, Oury said that psychoanalysis is a particular form of institutional psychotherapy.

---

[84] Evidence-based medicine: its exclusive supporters reject any medical practice that has not been scientifically verified. This is a reductive vision of medical practice: its exercise solely in the scientific process. If it is desired in all cases where it is possible, it cannot in any case be restricted to this single aspect without risking losing its humanity.

Cognitive behavioral therapies originate in education, and have little to do with previous psychotherapies, as they are derived from a mix between Pavlov, Lovaas, and others, and the Coué method, possibly influenced by an American-style psychotherapy of the ego, centered on the reconstruction of an autonomous ego in an essentially educational mode. I will not mention here operant conditioning, the "method" of which may be seen in Stanley Kubrick's *A Clockwork Orange*, a caricature in behavioral therapy. Psychotherapy is an *a posteriori* process, aimed at understanding experience as a whole, while cognitive behavioral therapy is an *a priori* process, aimed at normalizing a behavior.

Of course, education cannot in any way be summarized in these options, chosen by some only because it is easier to assess the apparent effects. An education worthy of the name is humanizing by definition, and educators with it. Limiting oneself to making the child, or even the dependent adult, acquire standardized behaviors is always liable to become a technique of influence if these methods are not transcended by the processes of identifications in the work of all intersubjective education.[85]

In intersubjective education, there is no opposition between these two approaches to the person, but, rather, the possibility of complementarities for those who deem it necessary. They respond to different needs, they obey specific logics, they must be able to live their lives independently, while coexisting without damage.

And even in the case of so-called cognitive behavioral therapies deliberately chosen by parents for the education of their child with autism, the working meetings between the actors of psychotherapy and those of the educational approach conceived in the transferential constellation, in the opinion of many practitioners

---

[85] Cf. François Tosquelles, *Hygiène mentale des éducateurs, conditions techniques et conditions matérielles* (1962), Paris: Éditions d'une, 2016.

open to these complementarities, provides evidence that it is possible for the whole of care to be humanized.[86]

In the development of the child, it is not necessary to be a rocket scientist to realize that education is partly at work in what structures his learning. But also, for a not insignificant part of his psychic construction, it is not the educational attitude that prevails, but *patheimathos*, learning by suffering (and the reflections it triggers), referred to in the world's attitude toward psychotherapy, which can be summed up by the question: "So you, little man! What do you think of this experience that we just went through together?"

It seems to me that the enormous conflicts that are currently at work in contemporary France, recently brought to the forefront by the unimaginable blunders on autism made by the successive ministers delegated to the disabled, consume a considerable amount of energy, revealing a reduction of thought to binary logic, and indicative of a radicalization of human problems and a gradual estrangement from a democratic atmosphere—without which psychotherapy cannot develop fully.

---

[86] Marie-Dominique Amy (dir.), *Autismes et psychanalyse*, Toulouse: Érès, 2014.

CHAPTER ELEVEN

By way of conclusion

The moment a society gives itself the right and the opportunity to ask these essential questions without immediately triggering senseless buzzes of disinformation and murderous thought-processes, there is a place for the subject to reside in man. After which—and this is the horizon of all freedom—comes the question of the anxiety that surrounds him. But anxiety is a hundred times better than deprivation of liberty. And if the anxiety proves to be too invasive, ferocious, or persecuting, then recourse to the psychiatrist and psychiatry teams is a response that society offers its members to temper their excesses. This is where the distinction between neurotic anxiety and archaic/psychotic anxiety finds its full justification, in so far as, as we have seen, the responses to them are not of the same order.

The idea of a modernity coinciding with a world where anxiety is no longer tolerated, where zero tolerance justifies a stifling precautionary principle extended to ordinary citizens, where boredom, the result of democratic disease and an early addiction to screens, must be banned, and where the expression of conflicts manifests a regrettable penchant for the spectacle, this anxiety therefore feeds the retreat of democracies in favor of post-democracy, which is nothing else than the integral of the figures mentioned above, what we have qualified as the "republic of false selves."

More than authenticity, it is the image one gives of oneself that counts in contemporary society, even if it means disguising oneself in order to seduce or manipulate—which, in fact, opens the field to perversions. However, in such a post-democracy, the opinion of the people is certainly collected as the proof of the existence of democracy; but their opinions are formatted by the media to appease the gods of consumption and the enrichment of international capitalism for the benefit of a few pot-bellied elites, and to the detriment of the "common."[87] One only has to look at the work of neuro-economics to see to what extent these hypotheses are no longer the political fictions of Huxley, Orwell, or Lewin, which we have loved all the more because they represented faraway and out of reach scarecrows. But in a few years, they have strengthened their hold over our cerebral unconscious, in the sense of Marcel Gauchet,[88] and undoubtedly also over our Freudian unconscious. False selves have now a bright future ahead of them.

Faced with such an observation that could pass for alarmist, all those among us who are carrying the project of restoring the subject in man (at the risk of a well-tempered anxiety) come up against these forces undermining basic humanism.

We must therefore resolutely face our detractors to oppose them with our stalwartness on the objectives pursued. Jean Cooren,

---

[87] Cf. Pierre Dardot, Christian Laval, *Commun*, op. cit.
[88] Cf. Marcel Gauchet, *L'Inconscient cérébral*, Paris: Le Seuil, 1992.

suggesting as the title for his latest work: *Other Could Be the World: Psychoanalysis and Democracy*,[89] thus summarized the whole of a re-humanization project.

To do this, it is not wise to reinforce the divisions between the different approaches to psychiatry. Rather, it would indicate to what extent our discipline cannot produce ethically acceptable results without support on the vision: "human first." The rectification of a behavior, if it does not include at the end of the day the meaning that its variations came to signify, is only valid as an acceptance to comply with the social norm in order to join the herd of almost-citizens of a media post-democracy, without words and with no future other than that of a veterinarian. It does not allow us to ask ourselves the question of the singularity of the people who make up our world, and even less to respond to the corollary anxieties which may result directly from it.

Finally, to return, by way of conclusion, to the exchange between Einstein and Freud, the latter, answering the former's question on the possible emergence of pacifism, declared in 1933:

> And now how long will it take for others to become pacifists in their turn? We cannot say, but perhaps it is not utopian to place hope in the action of these two elements, the concept of culture and the justified fear of the repercussions of a future conflagration, to put an end to war, in the near future. By what paths or detours, we cannot guess. In the meantime, we can say to ourselves: everything that works for the development of culture also works against war.[90]

---

[89] Jean Cooren, *Autre pourrait être le monde. Psychanalyse et démocratie*, Paris: Hermann, 2015.
[90] Sigmund Freud, *Why War? Letter to Albert Einstein*, op. cit.

Culture therefore remains our essential force against the deconstruction of our humanity, this new war that assails us.[91] And in the professions of human relations, we have an ardent desire for it to find its place where the imperialism of the number has set the pace of an announced surrender. Culture and democracy are decidedly the antidotes for a republic of false selves.

---

[91] Cf. François Cusset, *Le Déchaînement du monde: logique nouvelle de la violence*, Paris, La Découverte, 2018.

Index

active therapy, 13
    adhesive identity, 19–20
    alienation, 14–15
    "armored" syndrome, 19
    "burnout" syndrome, 19
    clinical example, 20
    dissociated transference, 15–16
    establishment and institution, 14
    insanity and social alienation, 14–15
    institution, treatment of, 13–14
    multireferential transference, 15–16
    phoric function, 21
    projectiles, 19
    projective and adhesive identification, 18–21
    Simon, H., 13–14
    transferential constellation, 16, 17–18
adhesive identification, 18–21
    see also active therapy
adhesive identity, 19–20 *see also* active therapy
Agamben, G., 76
alienation, 14 *see also* active therapy
    insanity, 14–15
    mental or psychopathological, 15
    social, 15, 82
    types of, 15
antipsychiatry, 25, 28, 42, 82
anxiety, 109–110
"armored" syndrome, 19
asylum, 43, 46, 88–89 *see also* psychiatric revolution
attachment theory, 71 *see also* "false self"
autism, 19–20, 28, 32–33, 35, 37, 42, 90–91, 108

Ayerdhal, Y., 78
Ayme, J., 94

Balint, M., 101
Béguin, F., 80
Bick, E., 19
Bonnafé, L., 81
Breaugh, M., 63
"burnout" syndrome, 19

care for mentally ill, 80
caregivers, 10–11, 14, 16–18, 19, 28, 42, 81
    distress of, 80
    experience, 33, 35
    and patients, 20–21, 35–36
    transference, 32, 96–97
carrying, 32 see also welcoming function
Chaigneau, H., 27
Clockwork Orange, A, 107
cognitive behavioral therapies, 99, 106–107
Cohen-Tanugi, L., 63
compartmentalization, 89 see also psychiatric revolution
contemporary child development, 72–73 see also "false self"
continuity of care, 35–38
    "complementary relationships", 36
    de-completeness relations, 36–37
    freedom of movement of patients, 36
    governing violence, 38
    patient circulation, 35
Cooper, D., 25
Cooren, J., 110–111
countertransference, 32, 33. See also welcoming function; transference
Crouch, C., 58

Dardot, P., 79
Debord, G., 76
de-completeness relations, 36–37, 38
deinstitutionalization, 41–42
Delion, P., 7, 9, 31, 35, 41, 69, 95, 96
democracy, xii–xiii see also politics
    institutions of, 58
    of opinion, 61
    system, 59–60
democratorship, 68
Deneault, A., 79
de Tocqueville, A., 60
dissociated transference
    see transference
Dufour, D.-R., 77

establishment, 9–10, 11, 14, 91, 95
    see also institution
evidence-based medicine, 102, 106

false self, 66–67, 68, 69–74, 75, 112
    attachment theory, 71
    development of contemporary child, 72–73
    double abnormality, 71–72
    good-enough mother, 70
    hypermaturity, 71
    id, 70
    image, 70
    me and self, 70
    morality, 72
    professional, 97
    psychoanalysts in, 97
    smile, 71
    Winnicott, 70, 71
flesh, 40
Foucault, M., 88
freedom of expression, 79
freeze-dried assessment processes, 85
Freud, S., 16, 70, 84, 90, 92
    Einstein and, 111

Freudian metapsychology, 88–89
Freudian project, 90–91

Gauchet, M., 63, 88
good-enough mother, 70
Gori, R., 97
Guattari, F., 23, 28

helping relationship, 79–82
    care for mentally ill, 80
    distress of staff, 80
    freedom of expression, 79
    hospital management, 81, 82
    isolated caregivers, 81
    social alienation, 82
hospital management, 81, 82
humanization, 83–85, 111–112
human psychiatry, 105–108
    evidence-based medicine, 106
    intersubjective education, 107
    operant conditioning, 107
    psychoanalysis, 106
    psychotherapy and cognitive-behavioral therapies, 106–107
human rights, 62–63 *see also* politics
hyperspecialized medicine, 101

id, 70
identification, projective and adhesive, 18–21
image, 65–68, 70, 110 *see also* false self
    faked, 97
    societal changes, 75–78
image inflation, 75–78
insanity, 14–15 *see also* active therapy
institution, 9–11, 14, 95 *see also* establishment; sector psychiatry
    emotion of staff, 31–33
    therapeutic club, 10
    Tosquelles, F. 14
institutional abandonment, 89
institutional analysis, 27–29
institutional psychotherapy (I.P.), xiii, 10, 23–25, 91–92 *see also* psychiatric revolution
    sector psychiatry, 43–44, 93–100
    the thing and the flesh, 39–40
intersubjective education, 107
I.P. *see* institutional psychotherapy

Julliard, J., 61, 66

Klein, M., 18

Lacan, J., 13
    theories of, 40, 70, 97
Laval, C., 79
Linhart, D., 81

Maldiney, H., 83
media, 65–68
medicine with human face, 101–103
Meltzer, D., 19
mental alienation, 15
Mermet, G., 68
metapsychology, 88–89
Miwaki, Y., 7
Möbius strip, 94 *see also* sector psychiatry
monarchical, 60 *see also* politics
morality, 72 *see also* "false self"
multireferential transference *see* transference
Murat, L., 88

narrative medicine, 101–102
neurosis, 90

oligarchic, 60, 62 *see also* politics
opinions, 65–68, 110

Oury, J., 13, 14, 23–25
    alienation, 15
    dissociated transference, 16
    patient flow and continuity of care, 35–38
    psychoanalysis, 106
    reception function, 31
    the thing and the flesh, 39–40
out-of-hospital therapeutic clubs, 46

patheimathos, 108
personal medicine, 102–103
Philibert, N., 39
phoric function, 21, 32, 95 *see also* welcoming function
politics, 57
    communication strategies, 61
    democracy of opinion, 61
    democratic system, 59–60
    giving back of power, 59
    human rights, 62–63
    institutions of democracy, 58
    maneuvers of leaders, 58–60
    manipulating citizens, 61
    oligarchy, 62
    position of representative, 58
    roots of clear conscience, 63
Popper, K., 60
projectiles, 19
projective identification, 18–21 *see also* active therapy
psychiatric revolution, 87
    asylum, 88–89
    compartmentalization, 89
    Freudian metapsychology, 88–89
    Freudian project, 90–91
    institutional abandonment, 89
    institutional psychotherapy, 91–92
    "mentally ill", 87
    "moral treatment", 87

neurosis, 90
psychiatry, 84–85
    anti-, 23–25
    effect of behavioralization of, 99–100
    human, 105–108
    public, 93–94
    sector, 43–44, 93–100
    secure, 84
    transferential, 84
psychoanalysis, 106
    free association, 57
psychoanalysts, 106 *see also* sector psychiatry
    in false self, 97
psychopathological alienation, 15
psychotherapy, 57, 107 *see also* institutional psychotherapy
    and cognitive behavioral therapies, 106–107
public psychiatry, 93–94

revolving door syndrome, 98–99 *see also* sector psychiatry
Rousseau, J.-J., 60

sector psychiatry, xiii, 43–44, 93
    effect of behavioralization, 99–100
    "complementary reports", 94
    de-medicalization of functions, 100
    faked image, 97
    innovative perspectives, 94–96
    institution, 95
    Möbius strip, 94
    phoric function, 95
    professional false self, 97
    professional healthcare team, 95
    psychiatrists and administrators, 98
    reality and image, 98

revolving door syndrome, 98–99
self-authorization, 97
transference logic, 96
transferential constellation, 95
working meetings, 96
secure psychiatry, 84
self-authorization, 97 *see also* sector psychiatry
"semaphoric function", 32, 33 *see also* welcoming function
Sextus Aurelius Victor, 59
Simon, H., 13–14
social alienation, 15, 82
social bonds, xii
socius, xii
spectacle, 76–77
spectator voters, 67
staff distress, 80
subject in man, 83–85, 94
Swain, G., 88

therapeutic work, 46 *see also* work and adaptation
thing, the, 40
Tosquelles, F., 13, 14, 83, 94
　establishment, 95
　institution, 14, 95
　multireferential transference, 15–16
　patient flow and continuity of care, 35–38
　re-socialization through work, 47
　therapeutic work, 46
　transferential constellation reunion, 16
transference, 15, 18, 32, 88–89, 90–91 *see also* countertransference
　adhesive, 20

dissociated, 16, 90
logic, 96
multireferential, 15–16
transferential constellation, 11, 17, 33, 95 *see also* active therapy; sector psychiatry; welcoming function
　and organizational difficulties, 17–18
　reunion, 16
transferential psychiatry, 84
transversality, 27–29

unconscious, 70, 90, 110

Vincent, C., 81
violence
　governing, 38
　transforming, 84

welcoming function, 31
　carrying, 32
　countertransference, 32, 33
　metaphorical function, 33
　phoric function, 32
　semaphoric function, 32, 33
　transferential constellation, 33
Winnicott, D. W., 71, 72
　false self, 66–67, 70
　holding, 32
work and adaptation, 45–47
　bogus work, 45
　false work, 46
　out-of-hospital therapeutic clubs, 46
　real work, 45
　re-socialization through work, 47
　therapeutic work, 46
working meetings, 96 *see also* sector psychiatry